MAYER SMITH

The Buried Pages of our Memory

Copyright © 2024 by Mayer Smith

All rights reserved. No part of this publication may be reproduced, stored or transmitted in any form or by any means, electronic, mechanical, photocopying, recording, scanning, or otherwise without written permission from the publisher. It is illegal to copy this book, post it to a website, or distribute it by any other means without permission.

This novel is entirely a work of fiction. The names, characters and incidents portrayed in it are the work of the author's imagination. Any resemblance to actual persons, living or dead, events or localities is entirely coincidental.

Mayer Smith asserts the moral right to be identified as the author of this work.

Mayer Smith has no responsibility for the persistence or accuracy of URLs for external or third-party Internet Websites referred to in this publication and does not guarantee that any content on such Websites is, or will remain, accurate or appropriate.

Designations used by companies to distinguish their products are often claimed as trademarks. All brand names and product names used in this book and on its cover are trade names, service marks, trademarks and registered trademarks of their respective owners. The publishers and the book are not associated with any product or vendor mentioned in this book. None of the companies referenced within the book have endorsed the book.

First edition

*This book was professionally typeset on Reedsy.
Find out more at reedsy.com*

Contents

#	Title	Page
1	The Unexpected Letter	1
2	The First Encounter	6
3	Whispers in the Dark	11
4	The Echoes of a Forgotten Promise	17
5	The Path Beneath the Moonlight	23
6	The Shadows That Follow	29
7	Echoes in the Silence	35
8	The Weight of the Unspoken	42
9	The Threads We Can't Cut	49
10	Beneath the Surface	55
11	The Heart Beneath the Earth	61
12	The Echoes of Lost Time	67
13	The Unraveling of the Thread	72
14	The Thread That Binds	78
15	The Heart of the Labyrinth	83
16	Echoes of a Broken Promise	89
17	The Unseen Door	95
18	The Veil Between Worlds	101
19	Echoes of the Unspoken	107
20	The Pulse of the Abyss	114
21	Beneath the Surface	120
22	The Weight of Silence	127
23	The Shadows That Follow	133
24	The Heart Beneath the Stone	139

25	Beneath the Veil of Memory	145
26	The Echoes of Forgotten Voices	150
27	The Unspoken Truth	156
28	The Echoes of Silence	162
29	The Secrets Beneath the Floorboards	168
30	The Echoes of the Forgotten	174
31	The Door That No One Should Open	179
32	The Weight of Forgotten Secrets	185
33	The Depths of Silence	191
34	The Echoes of Forgotten Dreams	196
35	The Path Beneath the Moon	202
36	The Veil of Forgotten Truths	208
37	The Last Whisper of the Past	214
38	Beneath the Weight of Silence	219
39	The Echo of the Forgotten	225
40	The Door of the Unseen	230

1

The Unexpected Letter

I had never expected to hear from him again. Not after everything that happened. The years had gone by—ten long years—and I had convinced myself that the past, with all its ghosts and unspoken truths, was buried deep enough to never resurface. But the letter arrived on a Wednesday, the kind of ordinary day that was supposed to pass without notice, like the ones that had followed the storm of our last meeting. I didn't recognize the handwriting at first. It was delicate, looping, and yet strangely familiar, as if written in the haste of someone trying to hold onto a memory that was slipping away.

I should have ignored it. I should have left it sealed, sitting on the counter where the mail pile had begun to gather dust. But the moment I touched it, I felt a chill run down my spine, a shiver of recognition, a pulse of something dark and unresolved.

With trembling fingers, I tore the envelope open. Inside, a single sheet of cream-colored paper was folded neatly in half, the edges slightly frayed from age. The ink was faint, the words heavy with an emotion I couldn't place. I took a deep breath and began to read.

"To Eliza,"

It started with my name, a name that had once tasted sweet on his lips but now seemed like a distant echo, a remnant of a life I had almost forgotten.

"I know you don't remember me. You never thought you would. But I'm writing because there are things you need to know. There are pieces of our story you never heard, and I need you to know them, whether you want to or not. I've waited too long to say this, but I can't wait any longer."

My heart started to pound, the words burning their way into my thoughts. You don't remember me. You never thought you would. How dare he assume I had forgotten him? How dare he suggest that after everything, I wouldn't still carry the weight of our time together? But then the next sentence struck me harder than I expected.

"I never meant for it to end the way it did. And I never meant to leave the way I did. There are things between us that were never resolved, and if you're willing to listen, I'll explain. I don't expect you to forgive me, but I hope you'll give me a chance to make it right."

The letter went on, but I couldn't read past those words. I never meant for it to end the way it did. A lump rose in my throat, and my vision blurred with the force of memories I thought I had locked away forever.

I hadn't heard from him since that night. That night—the one where everything had fallen apart, where our love had crumbled under the weight of the lies, the betrayals, the secrets. The night when I swore I would never let him back in, no matter the reason. And yet, here it was—his voice again, calling me back into a past I had worked so hard to escape.

I stood there, frozen, the letter crumpling in my hands as my mind raced. Was this a joke? Was someone playing with me? Could this really be from him?

I glanced at the return address. A name and an address I didn't recognize. A town I had never heard of. It was as if he had vanished completely from my life, only to reappear now, like a shadow emerging from the fog, too long gone to be truly real.

The world around me seemed to close in, the familiar comforts of my home suddenly feeling alien. I turned the letter over, but there was no more information—no signature, no explanation. Just the words that haunted me, that lingered in the air like a silent cry for help.

What did he want? Why now? Was I really ready to face him again? My heart fluttered in my chest, but it wasn't from excitement. It was from fear.

I had built a life for myself. A quiet, orderly life where I could forget the things I had once loved—and hated. He had been the storm that swept through everything I knew, and I had spent years trying to rebuild after the damage. I had convinced myself that time had healed all the wounds. But this letter... this letter was the spark that would ignite everything again.

I stood by the window, staring out into the night, my fingers still trembling as I clutched the paper in my hand. The wind outside was picking up, rustling the trees in the distance. The sky, once clear, was now filled with clouds, heavy and threatening. It felt like a warning.

I tried to steady my breath. Don't reply. Throw it away. Forget about it. But even as the thought crossed my mind, I knew it was futile. Something inside me was already moving, pulling me back to the past I thought I had buried.

Suddenly, the doorbell rang.

I jumped, the letter slipping from my hands and fluttering to the floor. I stared at the door, my pulse racing. I wasn't expecting anyone. Not at this hour.

I took a step forward, my feet cold against the floorboards. The doorbell rang again—longer this time, as if someone were waiting. I reached for the knob, hesitated, then pulled it open.

Standing in front of me was a man I didn't recognize. But his eyes—those eyes—I had seen them before. They were the same eyes that haunted my dreams, the eyes of someone I never thought I would see again.

And then, without saying a word, he handed me a second envelope. This one was sealed with wax, the emblem of a symbol I remembered all too well.

"Eliza," it read, *"If you're reading this, you're already too late."*

The air between us thickened, and for the first time in years, I could feel the past rising up to meet me. And I had no idea what to do next.

2

The First Encounter

I didn't open the second envelope right away. The first one, the one I had already read twice, still burned through my thoughts like an open flame. But this one—this one was different. It felt heavier in my hands, as though it carried something far more significant than words could express. The wax seal was familiar, and that sent a new wave of unease through me. That symbol. I knew it too well. It had been a part of my past, something I had tried to leave behind.

I stood there, holding the envelope, my fingers trembling slightly. The man at my door—the stranger with eyes I couldn't forget—had already turned and walked down the porch steps. He hadn't said a word, just handed me the envelope and left. No explanation. No name. Nothing but that silent departure, as if he knew I would understand everything once I opened the letter.

The wind outside had picked up again, rustling the trees and sending a chill through the air. I closed the door, locked it, and walked into the living room. The house felt empty now, even though I was alone. It felt like the walls themselves were holding their breath, waiting for something to happen. And I was waiting too.

The room felt colder, the air thicker, as I carefully ran my fingers over the wax seal. The deep crimson mark gleamed in the dim light of the room. I had seen that seal before—on letters I had once hoped never to read again.

With a swift motion, I broke the seal and unfolded the thick, heavy paper inside. The handwriting was unmistakable, as delicate and deliberate as it had been all those years ago. But the words... they were different. They weren't full of love or longing this time. There was something darker here, something urgent, something that made my heart race.

"Eliza,"

It began simply enough, but I knew there was more to it. There always was with him.

"You may not believe me, but what I'm about to tell you is the truth. The truth you have been running from. The truth you buried so deep inside you that you thought it was gone. But it's not. It's never gone."

I felt a chill creep up my spine. My breath caught in my throat. This was no ordinary letter. This was not just a letter from an old lover, apologizing or asking for forgiveness. This was a letter from someone who knew something about me—

something I hadn't even known about myself.

"You and I were always meant to be part of something bigger, something you've tried to forget. But the time for forgetting is over. You don't get to ignore this any longer."

I swallowed hard, my throat suddenly dry. What was he talking about? I didn't understand. What could he possibly mean?

"The time has come to face the truth, Eliza. And when you do, you'll understand why I had to leave. Why I had to disappear. But there's something you need to do now. Something that will bring you to the place where it all began. The place where our story started—and where it must end."

I froze. The place where it all began. I didn't need to read any more. I knew exactly what he was referring to.

The Cabin.

The words haunted me instantly, and with them, a flood of memories I had carefully locked away. The cabin in the woods, hidden from the world, the place where our love had bloomed, and where it had shattered. The place where so many things had happened that I had buried deep in my soul. It was where everything had started—and where everything had ended. Or so I had thought.

I looked up, the letter shaking in my hands. The room felt smaller now, the shadows in the corners of the room stretching toward me like fingers reaching for my skin. I had sworn never to go back there, never to let myself even think about it again. But now, the thought was alive in my mind, like a fire rekindling after years of being out.

I folded the letter carefully, my mind spinning with confusion and fear. But before I could process what was happening, the doorbell rang again, louder this time, with an insistence that sent another wave of panic through me.

I stood still, staring at the door. Could it be him again? Or someone else? My mind raced. I hadn't even had time to think. I could feel the weight of the moment pressing down on me. Was it time to confront the past? To face whatever had been buried in the shadows for so long?

The doorbell rang again.

I moved cautiously toward the door, trying to steady my breathing, but my heart was beating faster now, the blood rushing in my ears. I opened the door slowly.

He was standing there again. The man from before. His eyes met mine immediately—dark, unreadable, but there was something else in them this time. A flicker of recognition. A flash of something I couldn't place.

"Have you read it?" he asked, his voice low, almost a whisper.

I nodded slowly, still clutching the letter in my hand. "What is this? What do you want from me?"

He didn't answer right away. Instead, he stepped closer, just enough that I could smell the faint scent of tobacco and something else, something that reminded me of the woods. Of the cabin.

"I don't want anything from you," he said quietly. "I just need you to understand. There's no running from this, Eliza. You've been marked. And so have I." His eyes dropped to the letter in my hand. "That's just the beginning. The rest... it's already started. And it's coming for us."

I stared at him, feeling the cold air of the evening settle into my bones. His words sent an electric jolt through my chest, and I couldn't breathe.

"The rest of what?" I asked, barely able to speak.

"You'll find out soon enough," he said, then turned and walked away, leaving me standing there with the door half open, the letter still clutched in my hand.

I closed the door behind him, my mind reeling. His words hung in the air, thick with unspoken promises and threats. I couldn't shake the feeling that something was coming—something inevitable—and that I had just crossed a line that I could never return from.

3

Whispers in the Dark

The hours dragged on, but I couldn't shake the feeling that the world had changed. I sat in the dim light of my living room, the second letter still in my hands. I couldn't look at it again—not yet. My fingers trembled as I set it down on the coffee table, but I couldn't move away from it. The letter had unnerved me in a way I couldn't explain. The words were sharp, cutting through the fragile calm I had tried to build over the years. And the man—him—standing at my door again. He'd left so suddenly, like a shadow fading at dawn, but his presence lingered in the room, heavy and suffocating.

The silence in the house felt too loud now. It pressed against me, every creak of the floorboards, every rustle of the curtains, too noticeable. Too deliberate. I rose from the couch, pacing the room in an attempt to outrun the thoughts spiraling in my mind. What did he mean when he said "there's no running from this"? And what had he meant when he said, You've been marked?

I stopped at the window, pulling back the curtain just enough to peer outside. The street was empty. Not a single car drove past. The streetlights cast long shadows, stretching like fingers that reached out for me. I swallowed hard and turned away from the window. I had to think. I needed answers.

My phone buzzed on the coffee table. I hadn't even noticed I had left it there, but now it was impossible to ignore. I picked it up without thinking, the screen lighting up with an unknown number. For a second, I almost didn't answer, but something inside me told me that I couldn't avoid it any longer. The air was thick with expectation.

I swiped the screen.

"Hello?" My voice sounded distant, almost hollow.

"Eliza," the voice on the other end was familiar, but not quite. It was low, calm, and yet there was something strange about it. "I didn't expect you to pick up. But I suppose I should have known."

I froze. It wasn't the man from earlier. It wasn't even anyone I recognized. But somehow, I knew this voice, like an echo from a dream I couldn't quite recall.

"Who is this?" I demanded, my pulse quickening. "What do you want?"

There was a pause, a long, pregnant silence that stretched between us. Then, in a voice that seemed almost too soft, the person spoke again.

"We've been waiting for you."

A cold shiver ran down my spine. The words were cryptic, unsettling. Who was waiting for me? And why did it feel like I was being drawn into something far darker than I could comprehend?

"Listen to me carefully," the voice continued, its tone shifting to something more urgent. "There are things you need to understand. Things about your past, about what you thought you knew. About the man who came to your door." The voice hesitated. "He isn't who you think he is."

I closed my eyes, feeling the weight of the moment press down on me. The air felt suffocating now, heavy with the unsaid, with the things I had never wanted to confront.

"What do you mean?" I asked, my voice trembling despite myself.

"You have no idea how deep this goes, Eliza. How long they've been watching you. You're not just a part of this story—you are the story. The answer lies in the past, in the secrets you've buried. You need to find the truth before it finds you."

I shook my head, trying to make sense of the words. "What are you talking about?" I whispered. "Who are you?"

"I'm someone who's been trying to warn you," the voice replied.

"You have to leave. You have to get out of that house. Now."

"Why? What's going on?" Panic clawed at me, and my throat felt tight.

"Don't ask questions you're not ready to hear the answers to. Go. Now. Before it's too late."

The line went dead. The sudden silence was deafening. I stood there, phone still pressed to my ear, but there was nothing but the sound of my breath and the pounding of my heart. What the hell was happening? Who had called me? Who had been watching me?

I dropped the phone onto the coffee table, my hands shaking uncontrollably. The feeling of being watched had returned, stronger now, crawling under my skin. I glanced at the door, then at the window. My mind raced, my thoughts spiraling in every direction. Was it him? Had he sent this person? Or was there something more at play here than I could understand?

The house felt like a trap now, the walls closing in on me. I couldn't stay here. But where would I go? What if this was just some twisted game? What if they were watching me right now?

Without thinking, I grabbed my jacket and rushed toward the door. The sudden movement felt reckless, but I couldn't stop myself. I swung the door open, my breath coming in shallow bursts as I stepped out into the cold night air. My car was parked at the curb, but something told me I couldn't just drive away. I couldn't just run from this.

Then I heard it.

A sound in the distance, faint at first, but growing louder. A car engine. The low rumble of tires against asphalt. I stepped back, eyes darting to the street, my heart hammering in my chest. The headlights appeared around the corner, cutting through the darkness, and I froze.

It was coming for me.

I couldn't explain why, but I knew. I knew the car wasn't just passing by. It was headed straight for my house. Straight for me.

I ran back inside, slamming the door behind me. My breath came faster now, panic clawing at my throat. I pressed my back against the door, listening intently, but there was no sound. No footsteps. The car had stopped, but I couldn't hear it.

I crept to the window, my pulse racing. Through the curtains, I saw the car parked across the street. But no one got out.

I couldn't take my eyes off it. It was like waiting for something to happen, but not knowing what.

And then, just as quickly as it had arrived, the car was gone. Disappeared into the night, leaving nothing but a lingering sense of dread in its wake.

I stumbled back from the window, my body trembling with fear. It wasn't over. Whatever was happening, it was just beginning.

And I wasn't sure if I was ready for the truth.

But I was already too deep. And there was no way out.

4

The Echoes of a Forgotten Promise

The night stretched on, heavy with tension. I couldn't shake the images in my mind—the voice on the phone, the mystery of the man who had come to my door, the car that had stopped outside my house before disappearing into the night. Every detail seemed to fit into a larger puzzle, but the pieces refused to come together. I wasn't sure who or what was behind it all, but I knew one thing: I was being watched. And it wasn't just my imagination.

I paced the small, dimly lit living room, the silence broken only by the occasional creak of the floorboards. The letter from earlier still lay on the coffee table, its words haunting me, urging me to go back to the cabin. But could I trust them? Could I trust him? The man who had once been my everything had become a ghost—a whisper from the past that refused to stay buried. What had he meant by "you've been marked"? And why was I being dragged back into a world I thought I had left behind?

The walls of my home suddenly felt like they were closing in on me. I needed answers, but every path I considered seemed to lead to more questions, more shadows. I needed to talk to someone—someone who might have answers.

I grabbed my phone, hesitating for only a moment before dialing the number I knew by heart. As the phone rang, my fingers clenched around it, the uncertainty gnawing at me. The call went to voicemail. I couldn't leave a message—not yet. I hung up quickly, frustration building.

It was then that I noticed something strange. A faint tapping noise, like the sound of something lightly knocking against the window. My heart skipped a beat, and I froze. My pulse quickened as I slowly turned to face the window, but the curtain was drawn tightly.

I told myself it was nothing—a branch brushing against the glass in the wind. But deep down, I knew. Something wasn't right.

I crossed the room quietly, trying not to make a sound. As I approached the window, my hand reached out instinctively, my fingers brushing against the cold glass. And then—there it was again. A soft, rhythmic tapping, almost like a knock, followed by the unmistakable sound of someone breathing on the other side of the window.

I stepped back, my breath caught in my throat. I knew that sound. It was too familiar. It was his breathing—the same uneven, almost desperate sound I had heard countless times in the past. I backed away, my pulse racing, as I fumbled for the light switch.

The room brightened, the shadows retreating. I swallowed hard, trying to steady my breathing. But there was no denying it. The tapping had stopped. But I couldn't shake the feeling that someone was out there, waiting. Watching.

I took a step toward the window, my body tense, my heart hammering in my chest. Slowly, I peeled back the curtain, half-expecting to see a figure standing in the dark, a silhouette against the night. But there was nothing. No one.

I released a shaky breath, letting the curtain fall back into place. Yet the unease remained. There had been no mistaking the sound. Someone had been outside, close enough to touch the glass. But who?

My mind raced as I paced the room again, my thoughts spinning in all directions. What was happening? Was I losing my mind? Or was someone, something, deliberately pushing me toward something I wasn't ready for?

The phone buzzed again, jolting me out of my thoughts. I grabbed it, hoping it was the person I had tried calling earlier. But the number was unfamiliar.

I hesitated for a moment before answering. "Hello?"

"Eliza," the voice on the other end was calm, almost too calm. "I see you're starting to understand."

I froze, a cold wave of recognition washing over me. This was the voice from the phone call earlier. The same one that had warned me to leave, to run.

"I've been trying to tell you," the voice continued. "But you're too stubborn for your own good."

"Who are you?" I demanded, my voice barely above a whisper. "What do you want from me?"

There was a pause, a deep sigh, and then the voice spoke again, softer now. "The truth, Eliza. You need to understand the truth. All of it. And you're running out of time."

I felt a chill settle in my bones. My grip tightened on the phone. "What truth? What do you mean?"

"Go to the cabin," the voice said, almost as if it were a command. "There's something waiting for you there. Something you've forgotten. Something you need to remember. And when you do, it will all make sense."

The line went dead.

I stood there, the phone pressed to my ear, staring at the blank screen. My heart pounded in my chest as the weight of the conversation sank in. The cabin again. The place I had vowed never to return to. But why? What had happened there that I needed to remember?

I set the phone down, my hands shaking. I couldn't ignore it any longer. The man—the voice—whatever it was, it was all pointing to the cabin. But what if it was a trap? What if they were leading me into something I wasn't prepared for?

But then, just as quickly as the thought entered my mind, another one followed. What if it's the only way to get the answers I need?

I looked at the clock. It was past midnight, and the house felt impossibly quiet now. The weight of the decision hung heavy in the air. I had to go, didn't I? I couldn't keep running from this, whatever this was. The past had come calling, and now it was up to me to face it head-on.

I grabbed my jacket, slipping it on quickly. My breath was shallow, my pulse racing in anticipation. I had no idea what awaited me, but I knew one thing for sure—there was no turning back.

The cabin was only a couple of hours away, hidden deep in the woods. It had always been a place of secrets, a place where nothing was as it seemed. But now, it felt like the only place where I might find the answers I was desperate for.

With one last look at the empty, silent house, I turned and walked toward the door. Each step seemed heavier than the last, but I couldn't stop now. The past had its claws in me, and it wasn't going to let go.

I stepped out into the night, the cool air biting at my skin. My car waited for me at the curb, its headlights flickering as I approached. I opened the door and slid into the driver's seat, the engine roaring to life beneath my fingertips.

As I drove through the quiet streets, my mind raced with questions. What was waiting for me at the cabin? And why had it all been buried so deep for so long? I couldn't shake the feeling that something was coming. Something I couldn't stop. And whatever it was, I was going to have to face it—tonight.

5

The Path Beneath the Moonlight

The road to the cabin was long, winding through the dense forest like an artery carrying me further from everything I knew, deeper into the unknown. The moon hung high in the sky, its silver light flickering through the trees in soft beams, casting long, skeletal shadows across the road. I could feel the darkness pressing in from all sides, as if the woods themselves were alive, watching, waiting.

I gripped the steering wheel, my knuckles white, the engine's hum the only sound breaking the stillness of the night. The further I drove, the more the air seemed to thicken, until it felt like I was breathing underwater. My mind was a whirl of disjointed thoughts—questions I had no answers to, fragments of memories I couldn't quite place, and the eerie certainty that something was wrong, something beyond my control.

I hadn't been back here in years—ten, maybe more. Since that night. The night I'd left without a second glance, running from the wreckage of a life I had tried so hard to build. But the past had a way of catching up with you, didn't it? It had followed me all these years, silently at first, but now it was clawing its way back into my life, forcing me to confront it.

The cabin was close. I could feel it. I could hear the whisper of the wind through the trees, the murmur of the earth beneath the wheels of my car. But something else—something darker— seemed to be waiting for me just beyond the trees.

I turned onto a narrow dirt road, the tires crunching against the gravel. The path was overgrown, nature reclaiming the land as it always does, but it still felt familiar—too familiar. The old trees, the dense brush, the looming shadows—they were all part of the landscape I had once known so well. A part of me wanted to turn back, to leave the past buried where it belonged. But another part of me knew that I couldn't. Not anymore.

As I neared the clearing, where the cabin should have stood, a cold shiver ran down my spine. The headlights illuminated the abandoned structure, but there was something wrong about it. Something I couldn't quite place. The cabin looked... different. It hadn't changed much in all these years, but tonight, it seemed almost... alive. The shadows around it were too deep, too dense, like they were hiding something—or someone.

I slammed on the brakes, the car skidding to a halt in front of the cabin. My heart pounded in my chest, and I sat there for a moment, frozen in place. The silence was oppressive, like the world was holding its breath.

I could see the outline of the cabin through the windshield—

its sagging roof, the peeling paint, the broken windows. But something else caught my eye—a figure standing just inside the doorway. At first, I thought I was imagining things, but then the figure stepped forward, emerging from the shadows.

I didn't know who it was. The figure was cloaked in darkness, their features obscured by the deep shadows cast by the trees. But I could feel them watching me, and the sense of being known—of being observed—was enough to make my skin crawl.

I couldn't stay in the car any longer. I had to know who it was, had to know what was happening. But a small, rational part of my mind screamed at me to leave, to turn around and never look back. But it was too late for that. I was already here.

I opened the door, the hinges creaking in protest. The cold night air hit me like a slap, and I stepped out of the car, my feet crunching on the gravel as I approached the cabin. Every step felt heavier than the last, like something invisible was trying to hold me back.

As I got closer, the figure in the doorway became clearer. It was a man, but there was something unsettling about him. His posture was stiff, unnatural, as though he were standing too still. His face was obscured by the shadows, but I could see the outline of his features—sharp, angular. His hands were clenched at his sides, his fingers twitching like he was holding back something violent.

I stopped several feet away, my breath catching in my throat.

"Who are you?" I called out, my voice shaking despite myself. The man didn't answer. Instead, he took a slow step forward, his eyes glinting in the dim light.

Something about the way he moved made my skin crawl. He wasn't just walking—he was gliding, his feet barely making a sound as they touched the ground. His movements were too fluid, too deliberate, as though he were part of the darkness itself.

I took a step back, my heart hammering in my chest.

"Answer me!" I demanded, but the man remained silent. His gaze never wavered from mine, and in that silence, the air around us seemed to grow colder, the shadows deepening. I was aware of nothing but the sound of my own breathing and the soft rustling of the trees. The world had gone still.

And then, like a whisper on the wind, I heard it.

"Eliza…"

My name. Soft. Familiar. But there was no warmth in it—just coldness. And a hint of something else… something old. My stomach twisted as the voice seeped into my bones.

"Eliza… you've come back."

I froze, the air thickening around me. The voice was too familiar, too haunting. It was his voice—the man from my past, the man I had left behind. But how could it be? He had been... gone.

I shook my head, trying to clear the fog that had descended upon me. "No," I whispered, taking another step back. "You're not him."

The figure took another slow step forward, his eyes now glinting in the faint moonlight. His lips curled into a cold, almost predatory smile.

"No, Eliza," he said, his voice lowering, sending a chill through my entire body. "But I was him. And now... now, we are something more."

I backed away further, my legs weak beneath me. "What do you want from me?"

His smile widened, and he stepped out from the shadows. The full moon caught his face then, revealing features that were both familiar and alien. His eyes were hollow, empty, like they had seen too much, like they belonged to something that wasn't entirely human.

"I want you to remember," he whispered, his voice dripping with menace. "Remember everything. The truth is buried here, Eliza. And you won't leave until you've uncovered it."

I felt a wave of nausea hit me, and I turned to run, but before I could make it two steps, a hand gripped my arm, pulling me back. His grip was like iron, and I could feel the heat of his skin seeping into mine, sending a jolt of terror through me.

"There's no escaping this," he hissed. "The truth will find you, whether you like it or not."

And in that moment, I knew. I was trapped. The past had found me, and now there was no way out.

The ground beneath me seemed to shift, and I realized, with a growing sense of dread, that the cabin was no longer just a structure. It was part of something larger, something I hadn't even begun to understand.

I was about to learn what it was—and there was no turning back.

6

The Shadows That Follow

The man's grip tightened on my arm, pulling me toward the cabin with a force that seemed unnatural. His fingers dug into my flesh, cold and unyielding, as if he were trying to ground me in the earth itself. I could feel my pulse racing in my ears, my breath shallow and erratic, but I had no choice but to follow him. Every instinct screamed at me to break free, to run, but the weight of his presence was like a heavy hand on my chest, suffocating any thoughts of escape.

I stumbled along behind him, my legs weak, my mind a swirling haze of confusion and fear. The cabin loomed ahead, its broken windows reflecting the pale moonlight like hollow eyes watching me. The door creaked open without a sound as the man led me inside, the darkness inside swallowing us both.

The air in the cabin was thick, musty with the scent of old wood and decay. The silence was suffocating—too still, too heavy. I could hear nothing but the sound of my own breathing, quick and shallow, as I tried to make sense of everything that was happening.

"You're here now," the man said, his voice low and guttural. "You've come back to face the truth."

I didn't respond. I couldn't. Every word felt like it would weigh too much in the silence, like it would shatter the fragile sense of reality I was clinging to.

The man released my arm, but I didn't dare move. My legs felt as though they were made of stone, rooted to the ground by an invisible force. The cabin seemed to stretch out around me, its walls closing in, the shadows thickening, pressing in on all sides. I could feel something else in the air—a presence that was not just the man beside me, but something older, something much darker, watching and waiting.

"Sit down," he ordered, his tone carrying no room for argument.

I glanced around the cabin, searching for an escape, but there was nothing. The windows were boarded up, the only light coming from the weak moon filtering through cracks in the walls. The room was sparse, the furniture covered in dust, as though it hadn't been touched in years. And yet, there was something about it that felt... alive. As if it had been waiting for me.

I hesitated for a moment before lowering myself into an old, creaking chair in the corner. The man stood across from me, his eyes glowing faintly in the dim light, watching me with an intensity that made my skin crawl.

"Do you remember?" he asked, his voice soft, almost coaxing. "Do you remember why you left?"

I swallowed hard, trying to ignore the lump forming in my throat. The truth was, I didn't remember. Not fully. There were fragments, flashes of a life I had tried to bury, pieces of a story I had locked away in the deepest corners of my mind. But it wasn't enough. Not nearly enough.

"Why don't you remind me?" I asked, my voice trembling. I was barely holding it together, but there was something in his eyes—something that told me I wasn't going to leave until I knew everything.

The man smiled, a slow, cruel smile that didn't reach his eyes. He moved toward the center of the room, where an old chest sat beneath the window. His hands brushed across it, and for a moment, I thought I saw something flicker—just a flicker—in his eyes. A memory.

"This is where it all began," he said softly, almost reverently, as he opened the chest.

I could see the glint of something inside, something metallic. His hands moved with purpose as he pulled out a small, tarnished key. It was old, its edges worn from years of use, and yet it looked somehow... familiar.

He turned toward me, holding the key in his palm like a weapon.

"This key unlocks more than just the chest," he said, his voice low. "It unlocks the past you've been running from."

My heart skipped a beat. The key. I had seen it before.

"No," I whispered, shaking my head. "I don't want to remember."

But he didn't listen. The man moved toward me with the key, his eyes locked onto mine, and I felt something shift in the room. The air seemed to grow heavier, as though it were thickening with the weight of time itself. The shadows in the corners of the room stretched and twisted, as if they were alive, feeding off the tension between us.

"Too late," he said. His voice was barely above a whisper, but it reverberated in my chest like a low hum. "You can't run anymore, Eliza. You're already too far gone."

I recoiled instinctively, the walls of the cabin pressing in on me. The shadows seemed to grow darker, more menacing, wrapping around me like tendrils of darkness. I tried to stand, to flee, but my legs wouldn't move. The key was now inches from my face, glinting in the dim light, its presence suffocating me.

"Take it," the man said. "Take the key, and unlock the door you've kept closed for so long."

My breath caught in my throat, and for a moment, I thought I might suffocate from the weight of the decision. The key was in front of me, close enough to touch. But something inside me—something primal—screamed to resist. The memories, whatever they were, had to stay buried. I couldn't face them. I couldn't face the man standing before me, the dark figure whose presence seemed to warp the very fabric of the room.

"Please," I whispered, my voice cracking. "Don't make me do this."

But the man's expression didn't change. His eyes were cold, empty. He didn't care about my fear. He was beyond that. His purpose was clear.

"You don't have a choice," he said, his voice like ice. "You'll remember, Eliza. You'll remember everything."

I felt the cold, hard metal of the key press into my palm, and I could no longer fight the pull of it. Slowly, reluctantly, my fingers closed around the key. As soon as I did, the shadows around me seemed to pulse, as if the room itself were alive, reacting to my touch.

And then, before I could stop myself, I stood and moved toward the chest. The man watched, silent and still, as I inserted the key into the lock.

The click of the chest opening was deafening.

The air around me seemed to freeze, the silence so thick it was suffocating. My breath was shallow as I looked inside, and for the first time, I saw it. The thing that had been buried for so long.

A photograph.

My heart stuttered in my chest, my fingers trembling as I picked it up. It was faded, edges curling with age, but the image was unmistakable.

It was a photograph of me.

But there was something else. Someone else standing beside me.

And as I looked closer, my blood ran cold.

It was him.

But how? How was this possible?

I felt the walls of the room close in around me, the shadows thickening once more. There was no escape now. I had unlocked the door. And with it, I had opened something far darker than I could have ever imagined.

The past was no longer just a memory.

It was alive.

And it was coming for me.

7

Echoes in the Silence

The photograph trembled in my hand, the faded image blurring at the edges as my vision swam with disbelief. I had seen this picture before—many years ago, buried in the recesses of my mind. But it wasn't just the photograph that terrified me. It was the man standing beside me in the picture.

I knew him. I should have forgotten him. But I hadn't.

The cabin seemed to pulse with the weight of the memory, the shadows thickening around me as if the walls themselves were closing in, eager to swallow me whole. The air was too heavy, pressing against my chest, making it harder to breathe. The key—the one I had reluctantly held in my hand—felt like it was burning through my palm. But I couldn't let it go. I couldn't move.

I slowly lowered my gaze to the photograph again. There he was, the man from my past. His face was younger, his expression less haunting, but it was unmistakably him. And the way he stood next to me—too close, too intimate—made my skin crawl.

I hadn't seen him in years. I hadn't wanted to. He had been a part of my life I had buried deep, the part I tried to run from. But here he was, staring back at me from a photograph, as if he had never left.

I heard a creaking noise from behind me, like the shift of weight against wood. The hairs on the back of my neck stood up, and I spun around, the photograph still clutched in my hand.

The man was standing there, just inside the doorway of the cabin. His figure was still cloaked in shadows, his face obscured by the darkness, but I could feel his presence in the room. It was suffocating. Unbearable.

"You remember him, don't you?" The voice was like ice, slithering through the stillness of the room. The man's voice.

I didn't answer. I couldn't. The words lodged in my throat, too heavy to speak, as if the weight of them might bring the whole house crashing down around me.

"You don't have to say anything," he continued, his steps slow and deliberate as he moved into the room. His eyes, gleaming faintly in the dim light, never left mine. "I know you remember."

My heart began to pound in my chest, each beat louder than the last, echoing in the silence of the cabin. I could feel the room closing in around me, the shadows pressing against my skin, suffocating me.

"You should remember him," the man said, his voice softening, like a twisted lullaby. "He was your everything once. And you were his."

I shook my head, trying to block out the words, trying to block out the memory that threatened to resurface. "No," I whispered. "It's not true. It can't be."

But the man took another step toward me, and suddenly I was a child again, trapped in that same endless cycle of lies, of him—the one I had thought I could escape. The one I had thought I had forgotten.

"Don't you want to know what happened to him, Eliza?" the man asked, his voice dangerously calm. "Don't you want to know why he's not here anymore?"

I froze, the breath catching in my throat. I could feel the air shift, the temperature dropping, the shadows deepening. The walls of the cabin seemed to lean in, pressing me further into the corner, until I could feel the rough texture of the old wood against my back.

"No," I choked out, the word scraping against my dry throat. "I don't want to know. I don't want to remember."

The man smiled, and it was a smile that sent chills straight down my spine. He wasn't here to give me answers. He was here to make me remember.

"You don't have a choice, Eliza. The truth is already inside you. It's waiting to come out."

I turned away from him, the photograph still clutched tightly in my hand. My fingers were trembling so violently that I almost dropped it.

The past, the thing I had tried so hard to forget, was clawing its way back to the surface. And no matter how hard I tried to push it away, it was already here—alive and well, in the shadows of this cabin.

I tried to make sense of it. Tried to connect the dots between the man in the photograph and the man in front of me. Who was he? Why had I been so desperate to forget him? Why had he left? The questions tumbled through my mind like a storm, each one a weight I couldn't lift.

But just as the flood of memories threatened to break through, the man spoke again, his voice low and cutting through the tension like a blade.

"It's not him you should be afraid of, Eliza. It's you."

I turned back to him, confusion clouding my thoughts. "What do you mean?"

The man didn't answer immediately. He took another step toward me, his eyes narrowing, studying me like an insect under a magnifying glass.

"You'll see soon enough," he said. "The truth has a way of revealing itself when you least expect it."

A sound broke through the suffocating silence—a faint, distant scraping noise from the other side of the cabin. My heart lurched in my chest. Something was moving in the shadows.

"Did you hear that?" I whispered, my voice barely audible.

The man's gaze flickered toward the source of the noise, his face unreadable. "It's just the wind," he said, but there was a tremor in his voice—an uncertainty that sent a fresh wave of panic through me.

No. This was different. It wasn't the wind. I had heard the scrape. Something—someone—was in the cabin with us.

Without thinking, I rushed toward the door, but as soon as my hand touched the doorknob, the man's voice stopped me.

"You can't leave," he said, his tone sharp, commanding. "You're not allowed to leave until you've remembered everything."

I turned to him, my heart racing, and for the first time since stepping into this nightmare, I saw it—fear. It was reflected in his eyes, mirrored in the tension of his jaw.

He wasn't in control. Not anymore.

I swung open the door, not caring if I was making the wrong decision.

And then I saw it.

A figure, shrouded in the darkness of the woods, standing at the edge of the clearing.

It wasn't the man. This was someone else. Someone I couldn't place.

The figure didn't move. But I could feel its gaze on me, cold and unrelenting.

I tried to scream, but no sound came out. My throat was dry, constricted, as if I were choking on the truth. The shadows were closing in again, tighter this time.

The man's laugh—low and mocking—echoed in the distance, as though it were coming from every corner of the room.

"You think you can escape? You're not even close," he taunted.

And then the figure stepped forward, revealing its face.

It was mine.

It was me.

But it wasn't.

I stumbled backward, the room spinning around me, my breath coming in short gasps. The truth was breaking free, and I had no way to stop it.

The past had caught up with me. And there was no escape.

8

The Weight of the Unspoken

The door slammed shut behind me with a force that made the walls tremble. My pulse raced as I turned to face the figure in the clearing, still standing there—watching me. The air was thick, like a storm was rolling in, heavy with the promise of something unspeakable. The figure's presence sent a chill down my spine, its silence deafening in the night.

I took a step back, my feet unsteady, my mind racing. The woods seemed to stretch out endlessly around me, the trees twisted into gnarled shapes that loomed in the half-light like silent witnesses. There was no path, no clear direction. Only shadows. Only darkness.

The figure—me—didn't move. It just stood there, watching me with eyes that felt too familiar, too foreign. It was my face, but it was... wrong. There was something about it that didn't belong. The eyes were hollow, too empty, too dark. The skin was pale, unnaturally so, as if it had been drained of life.

My breath caught in my throat, my heart hammering in my chest. I tried to speak, but no words came. The air was thick with an oppressive silence that seemed to suffocate every thought I tried to form.

"Who are you?" I finally whispered, the question escaping my lips before I could stop it.

The figure didn't answer. It didn't need to. Its eyes spoke louder than any words could, and they were filled with an intensity that felt like a warning. A promise.

I glanced back at the cabin behind me, but the door was now shut tight, and I couldn't hear anything coming from within. Only the whisper of the wind through the trees, a sound so faint that it almost felt like a memory rather than reality.

The figure took a step forward, slow and deliberate. My body tensed, and I instinctively took a step back, but my legs felt like they were made of stone, rooted to the ground. The figure's gaze never wavered, and with each step it took, the distance between us seemed to shrink until I could feel its presence pressing against me, suffocating in its intensity.

I opened my mouth to speak, to ask it what it wanted, but no words came. The silence between us felt like a wall, an unbreachable barrier that left me feeling more isolated with each passing second. And yet, there was something familiar about the silence. Something I couldn't place.

"You can't outrun what's inside of you," the figure finally said, its voice not my own, but something distorted, like an echo from deep within my mind.

I flinched. My heart skipped a beat, and a wave of nausea hit me, as if the very words were poisoning the air. "What do you mean?" I forced out, but my voice cracked, weak with fear. "Who are you?"

The figure smiled—if it could even be called a smile. It wasn't comforting. It was chilling. A twisted, empty grin that didn't reach the hollow eyes. It was as if the figure knew something I didn't, something that had been buried for so long that it had nearly rotted away.

"You'll remember," it said, its voice like ice cutting through the stillness. "You'll remember everything eventually."

The ground beneath me felt unsteady, as though the earth itself was shifting, and for a moment, I thought I might fall. I tried to move, to back away, but my body refused to obey. I could feel my heart racing, thudding in my chest like a drum, and the world around me blurred as the figure drew closer.

With a sudden movement, it reached out, its hand—my hand—grasping at my wrist. The touch was cold, too cold, like the grip of death itself. I gasped, the air thick with panic, as I tried to wrench free. But the figure's grip tightened, its fingers digging into my skin with a strength that shouldn't have been possible.

"Let go of me!" I shouted, but the words were weak, fragile. They bounced off the oppressive silence, swallowed by the shadows.

The figure didn't release me. Instead, it pulled me closer, forcing me to look into its empty eyes.

"You can't run from what's buried inside you," it repeated, its voice almost soothing now, but with an edge that made my blood run cold. "You're already too far gone."

I tried to break free, to claw my way out of its grip, but it was no use. My vision blurred, and the world around me began to shift, warping, twisting into something unrecognizable. I felt as if I were falling, sinking into some dark, abyssal place that had no end.

And then, as if it were all some sick dream, the world snapped back into focus.

I was back in the cabin.

The figure was gone.

The air was still.

The only sound was the pounding of my heart in my ears.

I stood there for a moment, disoriented, my breath coming in ragged gasps. The cabin felt wrong. The walls closed in on me, the shadows in the corners seemed to move, to shift, as though they were alive, watching me. I could still feel the cold of the figure's touch on my wrist, the weight of its presence in the room.

I glanced around, but nothing had changed. The photograph I had found earlier was still clutched in my hand, its edges crinkling in my trembling fingers. I stared at it, my eyes tracing the image once more. The man—the one who had haunted my past—was there. But now, there was something new. Something I hadn't seen before.

In the background of the photo, barely visible, was a doorway. And in that doorway, a shadow.

A familiar shadow.

I turned away, dropping the photograph onto the floor as if it were too hot to touch. My head spun, my vision swimming with a mixture of fear and confusion. I needed to leave. I needed to escape.

I rushed to the door, my hands shaking as I fumbled with the handle. It didn't budge. The door was locked.

"Please," I whispered, my voice hoarse, broken. "Please let me out."

But no answer came. The silence was unbearable, more suffocating than before. I could feel the walls pressing in around me, the cabin shrinking with every breath I took.

I backed away, stumbling, my mind spinning with fragments of memories, pieces of a life I no longer recognized. The figure.

The photograph. The door. The shadows. Everything was connected, but I couldn't make sense of it. I couldn't grasp the truth, couldn't untangle the threads of this nightmare.

And then I saw it. The flicker of movement in the corner of the room.

The door.

The shadow.

It was there, just behind me, waiting.

I spun around, but the room was empty. Only the silence greeted me.

Except for the whispers.

They were there. Soft at first, like the rustle of leaves in the wind, but then louder. Clearer.

"Eliza…"

I froze, my blood running cold at the sound of my name.

"Eliza…"

The voice was low, familiar, and it came from everywhere. From the walls. From the floor. From the very air around me.

And then, a figure stepped out of the darkness, its face hidden in shadow.

It was him.

But this time, he was not a memory.

This time, he was real.

And I could no longer escape.

The weight of the unspoken truths pressed down on me. And there was no running anymore.

Not from him.

Not from what had been buried.

Not from the past that was now coming for me.

9

The Threads We Can't Cut

The room was cold. The kind of cold that seeped into your bones and made every movement feel like you were walking through molasses. I hadn't realized how long I had been sitting there, frozen, my back pressed against the door, staring at the empty space in front of me. The whispers had stopped, but the presence remained. It hung in the air, thick and palpable, like a storm that refused to break.

I glanced at the clock on the wall. The hands barely moved, as if time itself was reluctant to continue in this house, this place where reality felt warped and fragile. It had been hours since I'd found that photograph. Hours since the figure had emerged from the shadows. And yet, nothing had changed. I still sat here, in the same room, with the same walls closing in on me.

My thoughts were a tangled mess, each one more confusing than the last. The photo, the door, the figure. The whispers. It was all too much. The past felt like a bruise I kept touching, reopening the wound over and over again, unable to stop. Who was that man in the photograph? What did he have to do with me? And why had I returned here, to this place, after all these years?

I rubbed my temples, trying to calm my racing mind.

The door behind me creaked, the sound sharp in the silence.

I jolted upright, my breath catching in my throat. The door was still locked. There was no way anyone could have entered. Yet, the creak lingered, a question that hung in the air.

I turned slowly, scanning the room. Nothing. Just shadows and the faint glow of the fading light outside. I was alone. I had to be.

But I couldn't shake the feeling that something was watching me, something that I couldn't see. My skin prickled as the air seemed to grow thicker, more oppressive. It was like the room had grown smaller, the walls pressing in, inch by inch. I needed to get out. I needed to escape this suffocating claustrophobia.

I stood up, my legs shaky beneath me, and walked towards the window. The heavy curtains fluttered slightly as I pulled them back, but the view outside made my stomach drop.

The woods.

Endless woods.

I had been so sure I'd come to the cabin to find answers, to confront something buried deep in my past, but now it felt like the place was pulling me into its grip, suffocating me with its secrets. The photograph, the whispers, the man in the shadows—they were all pieces of something I couldn't see, something I couldn't understand.

A sharp knock at the door broke through my thoughts, freezing me in place.

Who was that? Who could be at the door?

I swallowed hard, my throat dry as I stepped back. I hadn't heard a car, hadn't seen anyone approach. The knock sounded again, louder this time, more insistent.

"Who's there?" My voice came out hoarse, barely above a whisper.

There was no answer.

The silence that followed was deafening, thick with anticipation. My heart thudded in my chest as I stared at the door, willing it to remain still, to not betray me. I was paralyzed, my mind racing with possibilities—none of them comforting. What if it was the figure from the photo? What if it was him, the man who had haunted my memories for so long? The one whose face I couldn't remember but knew deep in my gut I should.

The knock came again, but this time, it wasn't a simple rap. It was a rhythm, a pattern, like someone trying to communicate through the wood itself. My blood ran cold as I listened to the familiar, staccato beat. It was almost like...

It was almost like the sound of a heartbeat.

My breath quickened. The world felt unsteady, like the floor beneath me was tilting. The knocking stopped abruptly, and for a moment, everything seemed to freeze. The room was still, too still. I could hear my own heartbeat, pounding in my ears, deafening in its urgency. The door.

It felt wrong. It felt like I wasn't supposed to open it.

But I couldn't resist. Something inside me—the part of me that had been asleep for so long—urged me forward. My feet moved on their own, dragging me closer to the door. The air was thick, suffocating, and I could feel the weight of something unseen pressing against me.

I reached out, my hand trembling as it touched the cold doorknob. The instant my fingers brushed against it, the door rattled, as if something was trying to get through. The sound was sharp, almost violent. The wood groaned, and the lock clicked, as if it had been waiting for me to act.

I jerked the door open.

A rush of cold air blasted through the threshold, the smell of pine and damp earth flooding my senses. But there was no one there. No figure. No man.

Just the woods.

But something wasn't right. Something was wrong about this place. The trees stood too still, too silent, as if they were watching, waiting for something to happen.

I stepped outside, the weight of the unknown pulling me further into the darkening forest. My feet moved instinctively, like I was being guided by an invisible hand, and as I walked deeper, the whispering returned, soft at first, like the rustling of leaves.

"Eliza..."

I stopped dead in my tracks.

That voice. It was familiar, but it wasn't mine. It was the voice from the photo, the voice I couldn't quite place.

"Eliza..."

The whisper was closer now, clearer. It came from behind me. I spun around, my heart pounding in my chest, but there was nothing. Just the forest stretching on, the shadows deepening.

"Eliza..."

This time, the voice came from the trees, from the branches above me.

I could hear the rustling, the faint shifting of something moving within the darkness, but when I looked up, all I saw were the leaves, still and unmoving, as though the world itself had fallen into a deep, unbroken slumber.

I couldn't breathe.

I couldn't move.

But the voice kept calling my name.

It was getting closer now, and with each step it took, the air grew colder, the darkness heavier. Something was coming for me. Something I wasn't ready for. Something that had been waiting for me, for this moment, for this unholy reunion.

"Eliza..."

I couldn't run. I couldn't escape. The voice was everywhere, swirling around me, wrapping its fingers around my throat, squeezing the life out of me. I was trapped. Trapped in the woods. Trapped in the past.

I could feel it then. A presence. Not in front of me. Not behind me. But everywhere. Pressing in from all sides. Watching.

Waiting.

The whispers stopped. The voice fell silent.

But the darkness was closing in.

And I was no longer alone.

10

Beneath the Surface

The moon hung high in the sky, casting a pale, ghostly glow over the landscape, turning the woods into a labyrinth of shadows. I stood motionless, the cold air biting at my skin, but I felt nothing but an overwhelming sense of dread. The trees around me swayed in a breeze I couldn't feel, their leaves rustling in eerie whispers. And yet, the whispers were not the wind. They were... something else. Something that had been waiting for me.

I blinked, trying to clear my mind, but the memories rushed in, threatening to overwhelm me. The photo, the figure, the voice that called my name—Eliza. It all tangled together in a web of confusion and fear. Why was I here? What had I come back to?

The woods stretched out endlessly before me, the path ahead swallowed by darkness. There was no direction, no sense of safety. I was lost. I had to be.

"Eliza..."

The voice called again, this time softer, more insistent. It came from somewhere deep within the trees, pulling me forward with an invisible force. My heart hammered in my chest, the sound deafening in my ears, but my legs moved before I could stop them. Step after step, I ventured deeper into the woods, my breath coming in shallow, panicked gasps.

I tried to call out, to scream for help, but no sound escaped my lips. The forest seemed to close in around me, the space narrowing with every passing moment. My pulse quickened, a sense of urgency flooding my veins. The voice was closer now, as if it were right behind me, breathing down my neck.

"Eliza..."

The whisper was no longer a sound. It was a presence. A tangible force that tugged at the very core of me. I froze, my heart stuttering in my chest. I could feel it. Something was there. In the darkness. Watching me.

I turned slowly, my eyes searching for any sign of movement, but all I saw were the trees, standing like sentinels, their gnarled branches reaching for the sky. The moonlight flickered through the canopy, casting strange, elongated shadows that seemed to move of their own accord.

I was alone. I had to be.

And yet, the feeling of being watched only grew stronger.

The whispers continued, now all around me. It was as if the

woods themselves were alive, breathing, shifting, speaking in a language I couldn't understand. I wanted to run. To escape. But my feet were rooted to the ground, my body too afraid to move. I could feel the air growing colder, heavier, pressing in on me.

What did it want?

The question echoed in my mind, but it was quickly drowned out by another sound. A rustling. Soft at first, but growing louder, nearer. Something was moving through the underbrush. Something large. Something fast.

I spun around, my heart racing. But all I saw was the darkness.

And then, just as quickly as it had started, the sound stopped. The forest fell silent, too silent. The absence of noise was almost worse than the whispers, like the calm before a storm.

I stepped backward, instinctively seeking refuge. My mind raced, searching for something to hold onto, something that could explain the terror that clung to me. But there was nothing. Nothing except the shadows. The trees. The silence.

And then, from the darkness, something emerged.

It wasn't human. It couldn't have been. Its shape was distorted, its form like a nightmare stitched together from the very fabric of the forest. I couldn't see it clearly, but I knew it was there. I could feel it. Its presence was like an electric charge in the air, sharp and crackling.

The creature didn't move at first. It just stood there, watching me. Its eyes, if they could be called eyes, glowed faintly, like two pinpricks of light in the vastness of the night. It was taller than any human, its limbs elongated and twisted in unnatural angles. The shadows seemed to writhe around it, merging with its form, as though it were made of darkness itself.

I gasped, stepping backward, but the creature didn't advance. It remained still, as if it were studying me, weighing my every move. My body trembled, caught in the grip of terror. My thoughts scrambled for a way out, a way to escape, but I could see no path. The woods had swallowed me whole, and now it seemed they were ready to take me with them.

The creature's mouth—if it could be called a mouth—opened slowly, and from within it came a voice. Deep, guttural, and cold. The words were not in any language I knew, but they were unmistakably directed at me.

"Eliza..."

The way it said my name sent a chill down my spine. It wasn't the same voice from before. It was darker, heavier. And it was... familiar. Too familiar. A memory I couldn't grasp, a face I couldn't recall.

"Eliza..." The voice repeated, and I felt it inside me, a pulse of recognition deep within my bones.

I shook my head violently, trying to fight the wave of nausea that surged up from my gut. The darkness pressed in on me, the weight of it growing unbearable.

"Who are you?" I managed to choke out, the words barely leaving my lips.

The creature tilted its head slightly, as if considering the question. Then, without warning, it took a step forward, its long, twisted limbs moving with an unsettling grace. The shadows clung to it, wrapping around its body like a cloak.

I stumbled backward, my legs buckling beneath me. My vision blurred, and my breath came in desperate gasps. I didn't know what this thing was, but I knew it was dangerous. I had to get away. I had to run.

But my feet wouldn't move.

The creature was closer now, so close that I could feel the cold radiating from it, like the touch of death itself. I was trapped, unable to escape, unable to breathe. Its eyes locked onto mine, its gaze cold and knowing. It saw me. It knew me.

"Eliza…" it whispered again, the voice now a low hum that vibrated through the air, through my very soul. "You cannot run from me. You are mine."

The words echoed in my mind, a taunting refrain that made my heart stop in my chest. The shadows closed in tighter, suffocating me, drowning me in their dark embrace. I could hear the whispers again, louder now, surrounding me, filling my head.

"You are mine, Eliza."

And then, just as suddenly as it had appeared, the creature stopped. It froze, its limbs rigid, as if something had halted its movements. I couldn't understand why, but a strange feeling—something like an instinct—told me that I had just passed a point of no return.

The creature did not attack. It didn't move.

Instead, it simply waited. And in that moment, I realized something terrifying: the creature was not here for me.

It was here for something I had yet to uncover.

And I was the one who had invited it in.

11

The Heart Beneath the Earth

The forest had gone unnervingly still, as if the very air was holding its breath. I stood frozen in place, my body rigid with fear, the creature's glowing eyes locked onto mine. Time seemed to stretch in all directions, warping and bending under the weight of the tension. Every fiber of my being screamed at me to run, to escape, but my legs refused to move. I was rooted to the ground, the shadows of the forest crawling closer, as though they, too, were a part of the creature—its dark extensions reaching for me.

For a moment, there was only silence. The usual rustling of the trees, the hum of the forest's life, had vanished. There was no wind, no movement. Only the faint, rhythmic thudding of my heart, which seemed deafening in the oppressive quiet. And then, from deep within the darkness, I heard it—a whisper. Soft at first, like the faintest breath of wind, but growing louder, clearer.

"Eliza..."

The voice. It was him again—the one who had been haunting me, the one whose face I could never remember. But this time, it was not coming from the creature. It was coming from the earth itself.

I looked down, my chest tightening with dread. The ground beneath me seemed to shift, as if it were alive, pulsing with an energy I could feel beneath my feet. The soil was soft, damp, as though it had been disturbed. The whisper continued, now louder, almost urgent.

"Eliza, you have to listen…"

I tried to move, to step back, but my feet felt like they were cemented to the earth. It wasn't just the creature holding me here. It was the ground itself, the very soil beneath me, as if something was rising from the depths below, pulling me down with it.

Suddenly, the creature let out a low, guttural growl, a sound that vibrated through the air, a primal warning. It didn't step forward, but it didn't retreat either. It simply stood there, its eyes fixed on me, watching, waiting. And that's when I saw it.

A faint light. A flicker in the distance, barely visible through the trees. It was coming from the heart of the woods, where the darkness seemed thickest, almost impenetrable. But the light was there, pulsing, beckoning.

I didn't know why, but I felt an overwhelming pull toward it. The same force that had held me in place was now urging me forward, pushing me toward that light. It was not the creature, not the shadows. It was something else—something far deeper, far older. A part of the forest itself, perhaps, or something buried long ago.

I didn't want to go. Every instinct in me screamed to turn and run, to escape whatever this was. But my body was moving, taking slow, reluctant steps toward the light, each footfall heavy, as if the earth beneath me were trying to drag me back.

"Eliza, you have to understand..."

The voice came again, louder now, more insistent, but there was something else behind it. Desperation. A raw, pleading tone that cut through the terror, that twisted something deep within me. I couldn't place the voice, but it felt familiar, like the echo of a memory just out of reach, like something I should have known but had forgotten.

The flicker of light ahead grew brighter, clearer, until I could see it clearly—an opening in the trees, a space where the forest seemed to have receded. In the center of that space was a stone, large and ancient, half-buried in the earth. The light came from it, radiating outward in pale, ghostly beams that illuminated the surrounding woods in an eerie glow. The ground around the stone was cracked, as if it had been disturbed recently, like something had clawed its way through the earth.

I stepped closer, my pulse quickening. There was something here. Something I wasn't meant to see. But I couldn't stop myself. The voice, the light, the pull—it was all too powerful. I had to know. I had to understand.

"Eliza, listen to me..."

The voice was clearer now, no longer a whisper. It was as if it had moved closer, as if it were right behind me. My breath caught in my throat. I spun around, but there was nothing there. The creature was still in the distance, its eyes watching, unmoving. But the voice—it had been closer. It had been right behind me. I could feel it, like a breath on the back of my neck.

I took another step toward the stone, my hand trembling as I reached for it, the cold surface sending a shock of icy fear through my fingers. As soon as my hand made contact, the earth trembled beneath me. The ground groaned, like something deep below was awakening, stretching, coming back to life after a long, silent slumber.

The stone pulsed, glowing brighter, and for a split second, I saw it. A face. Faint, but there. It was the man from the photograph. The one whose face I could never quite remember. His eyes were wide, desperate, his mouth open in a silent scream. His features were distorted, twisted, as though they had been trapped in time, caught between two worlds. And then, just as quickly, the image vanished, swallowed by the stone's pulsing light.

A scream caught in my throat, but it was stifled by a sudden force, a pressure on my chest that made it hard to breathe. The voice came again, urgent now, sharp, almost frantic.

"Eliza, please! You have to stop! It's not what you think!"

I stepped back, my heart racing, my mind spinning. What was happening? What was this place? Why was the man in the photograph tied to this stone, to this voice? And why had I been brought here?

The earth shook again, harder this time, and the stone split, cracking open like an egg, revealing something inside. I couldn't see what it was, but I could feel it. The air around me had shifted, charged with something dark, something ancient. The shadows seemed to grow, stretching toward me, crawling along the ground like tendrils.

I stepped back again, panic rising in my chest. The whispers were everywhere now, filling my ears, drowning out all thought.

"Eliza... Eliza... Eliza..."

The ground began to tremble more violently, and I knew, deep down, that I was standing on the edge of something I couldn't understand. The man, the stone, the voices—it was all connected, but how? What did it all mean? I reached for the stone again, my fingers brushing against the cracked surface, and a shock of electricity coursed through me.

I jerked back, gasping, but the air was thick with the feeling of something about to break, something long buried and waiting to resurface. The whispers grew louder, more urgent.

"Eliza, don't..."

But it was too late. The earth shifted beneath me again, and the world seemed to tilt. And in that moment, I knew one thing for certain: I wasn't meant to leave this place. Not yet. Not until I uncovered the truth buried beneath the surface.

And something told me that truth was darker than I had ever imagined.

12

The Echoes of Lost Time

I couldn't remember how long I had been standing there, frozen in place. The stone was still pulsing with that unnatural light, the earth beneath it trembling with every breath I took. I wanted to run. I needed to run. But the force holding me in place, binding me to the stone, was stronger than any fear I had ever felt.

The whispers—those haunting, desperate whispers—continued, swirling around me like a whirlwind of forgotten voices. They were no longer distant, no longer echoes in the wind. They were in my ears, in my mind, and in my bones, pulling me deeper into the forest, into the very heart of whatever darkness lay beneath the earth.

"Eliza... Please... You have to listen..."

The voice was softer now, no longer desperate, but pleading, as if it had sensed my resistance and was trying to coax me into understanding. But understanding what? What could I possibly understand when everything around me seemed to be unraveling?

I took a step back, my heart pounding in my chest, but the ground beneath me shifted, as though the earth itself were pushing me forward. My feet moved against my will, dragging me closer to the stone, closer to the center of the pulsating light. My breath quickened, and for a brief moment, I thought I saw something—a shadow, or perhaps a figure—moving just beyond the edge of my vision.

I spun around, my pulse racing, but there was nothing there. Only the dark woods, the heavy silence that pressed in on me like a vice. The creature, the one that had been following me since my arrival in the forest, was nowhere to be seen. Had it retreated? Or was it waiting, watching from the shadows?

"Eliza..."

The voice again. But this time, it wasn't just one voice. It was many. A chorus of voices, all layered together, all speaking to me in a language I couldn't understand. The words were garbled, distant, yet each syllable seemed to strike deep within my chest, reverberating through my very soul. It was as if the forest itself was speaking to me, calling me by name, summoning me to something I couldn't yet comprehend.

I stumbled forward, my hand reaching out instinctively for the stone, the only thing that seemed to be tethering me to reality. As my fingers brushed against its surface, I felt a sharp jolt, like an electric current running through my veins. My body went rigid, my breath catching in my throat. And then, like a floodgate being opened, memories came rushing back.

Not my memories. Not the ones of my life in the city, not the ones of the mundane days I had spent before stepping into this cursed forest. No. These were older memories. Memories of a life I had never lived, of a past that was not mine.

I saw faces. Familiar faces, yet strange. Faces that had been lost in the shadows of time. I saw a woman, her face soft but lined with sorrow, her eyes pleading with someone—or something— just out of view. A man, standing tall and proud, his hand outstretched toward the woman, but his expression twisted with fear. And there, in the background, was the stone, glowing with the same eerie light that surrounded me now.

The vision flickered, changing, and I was transported once again—this time, to a room. A dimly lit room, where shadows danced on the walls, and the air was thick with secrets. In the corner, an old chest sat, its lid slightly ajar. I could feel the weight of something inside, something that had been buried for years, waiting to be uncovered.

The voices grew louder, more insistent. "Eliza... Eliza..."

I tried to pull away, to break free from the overwhelming flood of images and sounds, but I couldn't. The stone held me captive, its power stronger than any force I had ever encountered. The images of the past kept coming—faster now, more vivid, more real.

I saw the woman again, her face now twisted in terror, her eyes wide with fear as she whispered something to the man. The words were unclear, but the emotion was unmistakable. Desperation. A plea for help. A warning. And then, everything shattered.

The vision was gone, and I was left in the cold, quiet forest once again. My heart was racing, my head spinning from the intensity of the images I had just witnessed. I stumbled backward, my mind reeling, trying to make sense of what had just happened.

The stone was no longer glowing. The forest was still, unnaturally so. The only sound was the rapid beat of my own heart, hammering in my chest. I looked around, disoriented, but there was no sign of the creature, no sign of the mysterious presence that had been haunting me.

"Eliza..."

The voice came again, but this time, it wasn't from the stone. It wasn't from the air or the earth. It was inside my head, as if it had been there all along, waiting for me to listen.

The voice was familiar now, not a stranger's whisper but my own. I realized with a start that the voice I had been hearing was mine—my own, but from a different time, from a different version of myself. The memories I had seen, the faces I had witnessed, they weren't just from another life. They were my own. But why couldn't I remember them? Why had they been buried so deep?

I dropped to my knees, overwhelmed, my hands trembling as I dug at the earth in front of me, as if I could unearth the truth by sheer force. But the soil was cold, unyielding, refusing to give up its secrets. The stone, too, was silent now, its power spent, its glow faded into the night.

But I knew, deep down, that I had touched something far greater than I had ever imagined. The forest, the stone, the voices—they were all part of a much larger story. A story that had been waiting for me, a story that had been buried beneath layers of time and forgotten memories.

And the answers were just out of reach, hiding in the darkness, waiting for me to uncover them. But I knew one thing for certain: I couldn't leave. Not yet. Not until I understood what had been lost—and what had been hidden for so long.

I stood slowly, my hands still shaking, my eyes scanning the shadows. The forest was silent, but I knew it wasn't over. It was just beginning. And somewhere, deep beneath the earth, the truth was waiting to be found.

13

The Unraveling of the Thread

The air had shifted.

I had barely taken three steps away from the stone when the ground beneath me began to tremble. At first, it was a subtle vibration, like the faintest rumble of distant thunder, but it quickly grew in intensity, until the earth itself seemed to be alive with an ancient restlessness. The trees around me swayed, their branches creaking under the pressure of something unseen. The forest, which had been so silent moments ago, now hummed with a low, resonant sound that seemed to come from deep within the earth itself, as if the very roots of the trees were alive with whispers.

"Eliza..."

The voice came again, soft and urgent, but this time it was no longer a whisper. It was a command. It was no longer asking me to listen—it was demanding my attention, pulling me toward the center of the forest, toward the stone I had just left behind.

I stopped in my tracks, my heart pounding. I hadn't moved far, but it felt as though I had been transported miles away from the place I had just been. The forest had changed—grown darker, more oppressive. The shadows seemed deeper, as if they were thickening around me, closing in.

I turned back toward the stone, and there it was again: that pulsing light, still faint but undeniably present. The stone had not lost its glow. It beckoned me, its call growing louder, more insistent. I could feel it in my chest, a deep pull, as though the stone and the forest were drawing me into their depths, urging me to find what had been hidden.

"Eliza, come back."

The voice was clearer now, unmistakably mine, but not the voice I recognized. It was older, deeper, like the echo of a memory, a version of me I could not recall but instinctively knew. The sound of my own name sent a shiver through my spine. The air seemed to thicken with the weight of it, and I knew, without a doubt, that the forest was not done with me yet.

I took a deep breath and turned back toward the stone, my legs unwillingly carrying me forward. The tremor in the earth had grown more pronounced now, the ground vibrating beneath my feet. The pulse from the stone felt like the heartbeat of the forest, steady and constant, like a rhythm I had no choice but to follow.

When I reached the stone, the light was brighter, more intense.

I hesitated for a moment, staring at the cracks in the surface, the jagged lines that seemed to split the stone in half. It was as though the stone had been waiting, waiting for me to return, to complete something that had been broken long ago. And just as my fingers brushed against the surface once more, the earth shook violently.

I stumbled back, my hands flying to steady myself, but the ground shifted again, more violently this time. The trees around me groaned, their branches creaking and twisting unnaturally. It was as if the forest itself were alive, writhing in pain, struggling to keep something buried beneath the surface. The vibrations grew stronger, and the air thickened with an unbearable pressure. The stone pulsed, its light now blinding in its intensity.

Suddenly, the ground split open before me.

A jagged crack appeared in the earth, widening with a deafening sound, as if the very fabric of the world were being torn apart. My breath caught in my throat as I stared at the yawning abyss before me. The light from the stone flickered, its glow flickering erratically, casting long, distorted shadows across the forest floor. From deep within the crack, I could hear something—something ancient, something primal, a sound that seemed to echo from the depths of time itself.

The earth groaned again, and then, from the crack, something emerged.

It wasn't just a figure—it was an entire presence. A shape

formed from the shadows, from the dark recesses of the earth. Slowly, it began to take form, as if the forest itself were giving birth to whatever had been buried for so long.

At first, I couldn't make out its details. It was an outline, a mass of dark shapes, but as it slowly took shape, I could see it more clearly. It was a figure, humanoid, tall and shadowed, its features indistinct. The light from the stone flickered once more, illuminating the figure's form in a pale, sickly glow. Its face was obscured, shrouded in shadow, but I could feel its presence—its gaze—penetrating me, burning into me with an intensity that made my skin crawl.

It wasn't human. I couldn't explain it, but it wasn't human.

"Eliza…"

The voice called again, but this time, it wasn't mine. It was deep, otherworldly, like the sound of the forest itself speaking. It was older, ancient, as though it had spoken through time itself.

I stepped back, my heart hammering in my chest, but the figure—whatever it was—moved, slowly, deliberately, as if it was aware of me, aware of my every move. I didn't know what it wanted, but I could feel it, a presence that was suffocating, that made the air seem thin, almost impossible to breathe.

"Eliza, come closer."

The voice was compelling, hypnotic, and against every instinct, my legs began to move toward it. I fought it, but it was no use. The pull, the power, was too strong. I had no choice but to follow, my steps slow, deliberate, as though the forest itself were guiding me, directing me toward this strange, shadowed being that had emerged from the earth.

With every step, the darkness around me seemed to grow thicker, the shadows stretching and reaching for me, as though the forest itself were trying to swallow me whole. The air was electric, crackling with energy, and the ground beneath me seemed to pulse with life, as though something deep within the earth was awakening, stretching its limbs after a long, silent slumber.

When I was within arm's reach of the figure, it stopped. And then, for the first time, it spoke.

"Eliza, you are mine."

The words chilled me to the bone. It wasn't a statement—it was a declaration. And in that moment, I understood something. Something deep and unsettling. The forest had brought me here, the stone had drawn me in, and now, this figure—whatever it was—was claiming me, binding me to whatever dark force had been buried here for so long.

I opened my mouth to scream, but no sound came. My voice was gone, swallowed by the weight of the shadows, by the power of whatever ancient presence had now taken hold of the forest—and of me.

The figure raised its hand, and the shadows around us began to move, swirling like a storm, as if the earth itself were responding to its command. The ground trembled beneath us, and for the first time, I realized something terrifying.

I was not meant to leave.

Not now.

Not ever.

14

The Thread That Binds

The moment the figure spoke, the entire world seemed to collapse in on me. The words echoed, vibrating in my chest, sinking into my bones like a poison I couldn't escape. "Eliza, you are mine."

I tried to move, tried to take a step back, but the air itself held me in place, as though an invisible force had shackled me to the ground. My heart pounded in my chest, a frantic drumbeat that rang in my ears. I could feel the cold sweat trickling down my back, soaking into my clothes. My breath came in shallow gasps, each one sharp and strained, as if the very atmosphere had turned suffocating.

The figure—still shrouded in darkness—didn't move, but its presence seemed to grow with each passing second. The shadows around it twisted and spiraled, reaching out like tendrils, grasping at the air, as if hungry for something— something I didn't understand. The ground beneath me trembled again, and I felt a sickening pull toward the figure, a force more powerful than any I had ever encountered.

"Eliza..." The voice, now strangely soothing, beckoned again, but there was an undercurrent of menace to it. I tried to close my eyes, tried to block out the sound, but the voice seemed to seep into my very soul, wrapping itself around my thoughts like a vice. "Come closer..."

I struggled against the force that held me, my muscles aching as I tried to break free. My feet dragged against the earth, unwilling to move, as though the ground itself was pulling me back. But the pull from the figure was too strong, too insistent. I didn't understand why I couldn't break free. I had to get away. I had to escape.

But the shadows tightened around me, and before I knew it, I was moving, unwillingly, closer to the figure.

Each step I took felt like a betrayal. Every inch closer felt like a sinking feeling in my gut, like I was walking toward something I could never return from. The world around me blurred, the trees dissolving into a haze of darkness, the air thick with an oppressive weight. The figure's presence loomed larger as I neared, its outline growing sharper, more defined. The shadows surrounding it were thick, swirling like smoke, but I could still make out the faint outline of its face—if it could even be called that.

It was nothing like a human face, not in any way I could comprehend. It was a void, a shifting darkness that consumed everything in its path. I couldn't see its eyes, but I felt them—burning into me, like a pair of unseen forces that could see into the deepest corners of my soul. I wanted to scream, to call out for help, but my voice was gone, stolen by the weight of its presence.

"Don't resist," the voice said again, this time softer, almost tender. "You are the one I've been waiting for. You are the one who must set things right."

The words, though gentle, were wrapped in a thick layer of dread. I couldn't understand what it meant, couldn't comprehend why it was speaking to me like this. What did it want from me? Why was I the one being chosen?

I stopped, just a few feet away from the figure now. The shadows curled around me, brushing against my skin, cold as ice. The air smelled of damp earth and something sweet, like decay. My breath caught in my throat as the figure's presence seemed to press down on me, suffocating me with its weight.

"Why me?" I whispered, the words barely escaping my lips. I couldn't help myself, the question bursting out despite my fear. "What do you want from me?"

The figure didn't answer immediately. It remained silent, still as stone, its form pulsating with a dark energy that seemed to pulse in rhythm with the beating of my heart. And then, slowly, as though the words had to be dragged from it, it spoke.

"You are the key, Eliza. The thread that binds us all. Without you, there can be no balance. Without you, there is only the endless cycle of suffering."

I felt the words like a blow, heavy and incomprehensible. What did it mean? What cycle? And how was I the key? The questions swirled in my mind, faster and faster, but I couldn't grasp any of them. They slipped away like sand through my fingers, always just out of reach.

Suddenly, the ground beneath me cracked, and a low rumble vibrated through the earth. The crack widened, and I stumbled back, instinctively, only to find myself trapped. The shadows around me seemed to reach for my legs, pulling me toward the gaping chasm in the ground. I fought against it, kicking and thrashing, but the force of the shadows was too much.

"Eliza..." The voice grew louder, more insistent, its tone

almost impatient now. "Do not resist. You have no choice. The thread must be pulled."

I looked down, and for the first time, I saw it—a faint glow beneath the soil, pulsing in time with the rhythm of the figure's words. The glow grew brighter, and I realized with a sinking feeling that it was a thread, winding its way through the earth, entwining itself with the roots of the trees, binding everything in this forest together.

The thread—the key.

My mind was a whirlwind of confusion, but I knew one thing for certain. The thread was me. It had to be. The forest, the figure, the stone—it had all been waiting for me. I had been drawn here, led by forces I couldn't understand. And now, I was standing at the very center of it all.

"You must let go," the figure whispered, its voice no longer comforting but commanding, demanding. "Let go, Eliza. Let the thread unravel."

I felt the earth beneath me shifting again, the vibrations growing stronger, the ground cracking wider, threatening to swallow me whole. My body trembled, my limbs weak and unsteady, as if I were no longer in control. The thread—whatever it was—was pulling me, drawing me toward it, and I had no choice but to follow.

"Let go," the figure repeated, its voice low and soothing, like a lullaby, like a final warning. "Let it all unravel, and you will understand."

I took a step back, my foot slipping on the uneven ground, but before I could regain my balance, the shadows surged forward, grabbing hold of me, pulling me closer to the crack in the earth. The thread, now visible beneath the soil, glowed with an otherworldly light, illuminating the darkness with an eerie, unsettling glow.

And then, just as I was about to be swallowed by the shadows, a new voice—one that was both familiar and strange—whispered in my ear.

"Run, Eliza. Run."

It was my voice. But it wasn't my voice. And in that moment, I understood. The forest had been waiting for me to remember. The figure was not the only force at work here. There was another. And I had to find it.

I had to find the strength to break the thread. Before it unraveled everything.

15

The Heart of the Labyrinth

I could feel it now—the weight of the decision pressing against me like a stone lodged deep in my chest. The path ahead, though shrouded in darkness, called to me with an irresistible pull. But I knew better than to trust it. I had learned the hard way that some paths, no matter how enticing, lead only to more shadows.

The labyrinth of trees and tangled branches had become my prison, its walls tightening with each step I took. Every direction felt like a dead-end, every turn a futile attempt to escape. The murmurs of the forest—soft whispers on the wind—seemed to guide me, or perhaps mislead me, each whisper a riddle I could not solve. I had tried to run, to find the way out, but the more I struggled, the more the maze seemed to twist around me, as if it were alive, watching, waiting.

I glanced over my shoulder, half-expecting to see the figure—its haunting presence still looming in the corners of my mind. But the shadows were silent now, as though the forest itself had swallowed the sound of its steps. The figure had vanished, leaving me with only its words, echoing in my mind: You are the key. Let it unravel.

A cold shiver ran down my spine, and I quickened my pace, desperation creeping into my every move. My heart hammered in my chest, each beat a reminder of how close I had come to losing myself in that darkness.

The air grew thicker, as if the very atmosphere had been laced with something poisonous, something ancient. I stumbled over roots that seemed to shift beneath my feet, each step more treacherous than the last. The trees around me loomed like silent sentinels, their twisted branches reaching toward me, their bark slick and blackened as though they had absorbed years of suffering.

Then I heard it.

A sound, faint at first, but unmistakable: the rustling of leaves. Soft, deliberate, as though someone—something—was moving through the forest with purpose. My breath caught in my throat, and I stopped dead in my tracks. The shadows seemed to stretch, reaching toward me, thick and heavy, as though the very darkness was alive.

I held my breath, straining to hear more, but the sound stopped abruptly. My instincts screamed at me to move, to keep going, to escape whatever it was that lurked just beyond my sight. But my body betrayed me. I couldn't move. I stood frozen, my eyes darting from one shadow to the next, waiting for something, anything, to give away the creature's location.

The rustling began again, this time closer, much closer. My heart pounded in my ears, my pulse thrumming with fear. I wanted to scream, to call out, but the words stuck in my throat. Every instinct told me to run, but the labyrinth held me in its grip.

Then, through the murky darkness, I saw it—two glowing orbs, hovering in the distance, like eyes watching from the void. They blinked slowly, deliberately, as if they were studying me. My breath caught, my chest tightening with terror. I wanted to turn and flee, but my legs refused to obey. The eyes stayed fixed on me, unmoving, and in that moment, I realized they were not human. The shape that followed them was too large, too unnatural.

The ground beneath me trembled, a low rumble shaking the earth. I felt it in my bones, a primal warning, and before I could react, the thing emerged from the shadows.

It was a creature unlike anything I had ever seen. Its body was elongated and dark, moving like a shadow but with the solidity of flesh. Its eyes—those burning, glowing orbs—locked onto mine with an intensity that sent a wave of nausea through me. It was almost... human, but not quite. Its limbs were too long, its movements too fluid, like something that didn't belong in this world.

I gasped, taking a step back, but my foot caught on a root, and I tumbled to the ground. My heart was a drumbeat in my chest, my breath coming in short, panicked bursts. The creature's gaze never wavered as it slowly approached, its long limbs making no sound as they brushed against the earth.

"Eliza," the voice came again, this time from the creature, its tone chillingly familiar, "I've been waiting for you."

The words echoed in my mind, stirring a memory I couldn't quite grasp. I shook my head, trying to clear it, but the more I thought, the more the edges of the memory blurred, slipping further away, like sand through my fingers.

"Who... Who are you?" I managed to whisper, my voice shaking.

The creature stopped just a few feet away, its body casting a shadow over me. It tilted its head, as though considering my question. Then, in a voice that sounded both old and new, it spoke again.

"Does it matter? You know me. You've always known me."

The words hit me like a wave. Something about them stirred deep within me, a recognition I couldn't place. My mind scrambled, reaching for the connection, but it was elusive, just out of reach.

The creature took another step closer, its presence overwhelming. It loomed over me like a dark cloud, its cold eyes never leaving mine. The whispers of the forest seemed to grow louder, and I could hear something else beneath them, something deeper—an ancient hum, vibrating through the very air.

"You are the key," the creature repeated, its voice now tinged with a strange mixture of patience and desperation. "Only you can end it, Eliza."

I didn't understand. What was it talking about? What was ending? My mind was racing, the words tumbling over each other, but nothing made sense.

"What do you mean?" I demanded, pushing myself up from the ground, my hands trembling. "What do you want from me?"

The creature's glowing eyes softened, the strange intensity of them fading slightly. "I want nothing from you, Eliza. But you—" it leaned in closer, its breath cold against my skin, "you are the one who can stop it all. You are the one who can unlock the truth."

I recoiled, my mind reeling. The truth? What truth?

The creature stepped back, its form shifting, becoming less distinct, as though the very shadows around it were part of its being.

"You have come too far to turn back," it said, its voice now a mere whisper. "The labyrinth will not let you leave until you choose."

I swallowed hard, my pulse racing. I had no choice. I couldn't leave. I had to keep moving forward.

"Find the heart of the labyrinth," the creature murmured, as it slowly began to fade into the shadows. "Find what binds us all together. And when you do, you will know what to do."

And then, just as suddenly as it had appeared, the creature vanished, leaving me standing alone in the darkness, the weight of its words pressing down on me.

The labyrinth, still endless and twisting, stretched before me. I had no idea what I was looking for, but I knew one thing with certainty now: I could not stop. The heart of the labyrinth awaited me, and only there would I find the answers I so desperately needed.

16

Echoes of a Broken Promise

The air was colder now, biting at my skin like a thousand unseen needles. I had lost track of time in the labyrinth, the days bleeding together into an endless night. My thoughts felt like a fog, swirling and disjointed, each step forward an effort to clear the mist. Yet, it only thickened. The creature's words echoed in my mind, louder with every passing moment.

"You are the one who can unlock the truth."

What truth? What did it mean? The more I thought about it, the more my mind screamed to stop, to forget about this place, this journey, this madness. But I couldn't. It wasn't just the labyrinth that held me captive; it was something deeper, something old and buried beneath years of silence. A promise—no, a betrayal—that I had made long ago.

I stumbled forward, my feet dragging against the uneven ground, my body aching from exhaustion. The darkness around me seemed to close in tighter with every step, pressing in like a vice, suffocating the air from my lungs. There was no sound in the labyrinth anymore, no whispers, no rustling. Just silence.

But then, just as I was about to give in to the overwhelming despair, a faint light flickered in the distance. I froze. My heart skipped a beat. Could it be? Was I finally nearing the end? The light shimmered faintly, almost as if teasing me, daring me to follow.

I didn't hesitate. I pushed myself forward, my legs burning with each stride, the light pulling me in like a moth to a flame. The ground beneath me seemed to shift, as if the labyrinth was alive, reshaping itself with each passing moment. But the light didn't move, didn't waver. It was steady, constant, a beacon in the vast sea of darkness.

I reached the source of the light in what felt like an eternity, my heart hammering in my chest, my breath ragged. And there, in the middle of a small clearing, was a stone pedestal, ancient and covered in moss, a single candle flickering atop it.

The flame burned brightly, but there was something wrong about it. The light didn't seem to reach the edges of the clearing. It hovered unnaturally, as if it were trapped within an invisible barrier. I stepped closer, my hand instinctively reaching out to touch the flame, but before I could, a voice broke the silence.

"Eliza."

The voice sent a chill down my spine. It was familiar—too familiar. My hand froze in midair. It wasn't just a voice; it was his voice.

I whipped around, my heart crashing against my ribs. And there he was. Standing just beyond the flickering light, his face obscured in shadow, but his presence unmistakable. The man I had been running from for so long.

"Derek?" My voice trembled, disbelief rising in my chest. "How—how did you—?"

"You're not meant to be here," he interrupted, his voice low, almost a growl. He took a step forward, but the light held him back, creating a barrier between us.

I blinked, trying to understand what was happening. Derek's eyes, those hauntingly familiar eyes, stared at me with an intensity that made my skin crawl. The same eyes I had once trusted—eyes that had once been the only thing I believed in.

"I've been waiting for you," he said again, his voice thick with something I couldn't quite place. It was neither anger nor sadness, but something darker, more menacing.

"Why?" I asked, my voice barely a whisper. I was shaking, but not just from fear. There was a knot in my stomach, a sickening feeling that twisted and pulled at the edges of my mind.

He didn't answer right away. Instead, he stepped closer, his movements deliberate, as if measuring each step carefully. "You broke the promise," he finally said, his words slow, weighted.

My pulse quickened, my breath caught in my throat. "What promise?" I asked, trying to steady myself. But I knew. Deep down, I knew exactly what he was talking about. The promise I had made all those years ago. The promise I had broken.

"You were supposed to forget me," he continued, his eyes narrowing as he moved closer. "You were supposed to let it go. But you chose to remember, Eliza. And now we're both trapped here."

I could feel the weight of his words, pressing down on me, suffocating me. "I didn't choose this," I whispered, stepping back. My mind raced, trying to piece together the fragments of memories that had eluded me for so long. Derek... he wasn't just a man from my past. He was something more. Something else.

"You never understood," Derek said, his voice laced with bitterness. "You never understood the power of what we had. The bond. The promise. It was never just about us."

The air around us seemed to thicken, the light from the candle flickering violently. I looked back at it, but it wasn't the same. The flame was no longer warm, no longer inviting. It was dark, pulsating with an ominous energy that made my blood run cold.

"You knew what would happen if you remembered," Derek continued, his voice rising, the shadows around him deepening. "And now, it's too late."

I could barely breathe as the realization hit me. The labyrinth wasn't just a place. It was a prison—a prison created by the promise I had made to forget, to let go of everything tied to Derek. But now, I was here, in this twisted place, with no way to escape.

I took another step back, my body shaking uncontrollably. "I didn't know," I said, my voice barely audible. "I didn't know what it would cost."

"You should have," Derek said, his eyes now glowing with an unnatural light. His form flickered, like a shadow that couldn't stay still. "And now, you're going to pay for it."

I turned to run, but the labyrinth had shifted again. The walls, once distant, now closed in, trapping me. The light from the candle flickered one last time before it went out completely, plunging me into a suffocating darkness.

The sound of Derek's voice echoed in the emptiness, louder now, closer. "You can't escape, Eliza. Not this time."

I spun around, my heart pounding, my breath ragged. The darkness was thick, pressing in from all sides. And yet, in the distance, I could see him—his face now fully illuminated by the sickly glow of the shadows.

The walls of the labyrinth were closing in, and I knew, with a chilling certainty, that there was no way out. Not unless I made a choice. Not unless I faced the truth of what I had done.

And that truth—was buried deeper than I could ever imagine.

17

The Unseen Door

The air in the labyrinth had thickened again, growing heavy with a strange kind of stillness. The darkness seemed to pulse with a rhythm, a heartbeat that echoed in my chest. I could still hear Derek's voice, a low murmur in the distance, but it felt like it was coming from everywhere, drowning me in its weight.

"You can't escape," his voice whispered, the words seeping into my skin, tugging at something deep within me. "You'll never be free of this place."

I clenched my fists, my breath shallow as I tried to focus, tried to gather my thoughts in the overwhelming chaos of my mind. The labyrinth seemed to stretch endlessly in all directions, but now, it felt different. The walls, which had once been an unpredictable maze, now seemed purposeful, their shadows curling in on themselves, closing me in.

But then, just as I was about to give in to the madness creeping in at the edges of my mind, I noticed it.

A door.

It was barely visible, almost as if it had been hidden in plain sight, camouflaged against the walls of the labyrinth. It wasn't much—just a faint outline in the darkness, but it was there, waiting for me. A door that had not been there moments ago.

I stepped forward cautiously, my heart racing as my eyes darted from one shadow to the next. Could it be real? Could it be the way out? Or was it another illusion, a cruel trick of the labyrinth designed to lead me deeper into its endless maze?

The moment my hand brushed against the doorframe, the world around me seemed to shift. The labyrinth seemed to breathe—deep, slow inhales that filled my lungs with cold air. The shadows, which had once seemed so thick and suffocating, now parted ever so slightly, as though they were drawn back by the touch of the door.

I hesitated. There was a gnawing feeling in my gut, an instinct telling me that something wasn't right. This door—this entrance—did not belong here. It felt too easy, too sudden. I could hear the faint hum of electricity, a low whirring sound behind the door, like the machinery of some ancient engine awakening.

But something pushed me forward. The weight of Derek's words still pressed against me, wrapping around my mind, suffocating me with their cold logic. You'll never be free.

No. I refused to accept that. I refused to believe that the

labyrinth would claim me, that Derek's voice would be the last thing I heard. I had to fight. I had to make it out. I had to find the truth.

I placed my hand on the door's cold surface, feeling the smoothness of the metal beneath my fingertips. The door was solid, unyielding—no crack, no seam. But as I pressed against it, I felt it shift, the slight give of the mechanism hidden behind its surface. A soft click echoed in the stillness, and with a deep breath, I pushed the door open.

It was as though I had crossed into another world.

The air changed immediately, shifting from the heavy, suffocating weight of the labyrinth to a strange lightness, almost ethereal. The darkness was gone. Instead, I was standing in a large, open space. I blinked in confusion, my eyes adjusting to the sudden brightness of the room.

The space was vast, more vast than anything I had encountered within the maze. The walls stretched upward, far beyond my sight, disappearing into an unseen sky. The floor beneath me was smooth, almost reflective, as if made from glass, and it pulsed with a soft, undulating light that seemed to come from nowhere and everywhere at once.

In the center of the room, there was a pedestal. On it sat a book—old, its leather cover cracked and worn with age. But it was not the book that caught my attention. It was the strange, shimmering symbols etched into the floor around the pedestal, glowing faintly, like constellations from some other world. I felt a chill crawl down my spine as I gazed at them. The symbols were familiar, their shapes curling and twisting in ways that made my stomach turn.

I took a hesitant step forward, my mind racing. This place—this room—it was not a part of the labyrinth. I had crossed through something, passed through a threshold that shouldn't exist.

The book beckoned to me, its presence pulling me toward it like a magnet. My hands shook as I reached out for it, my fingers brushing the cool surface of the cover. I hesitated just a moment before lifting it, feeling the weight of it settle into my hands. The symbols beneath the pedestal seemed to pulse faster, brighter, as if reacting to the touch of the book.

I opened it.

The pages were blank at first, empty, save for a single line of text scrawled in a jagged, unfamiliar script. I couldn't read it—not at first. But as my fingers hovered over the words, they shifted, changing into something I could understand.

The truth lies within the heart of the labyrinth.

The words sent a tremor through me. My breath hitched, and for a moment, the world around me seemed to blur. What was this? What was this place? And why had the book led me here?

Before I could comprehend it fully, I heard it—the sound of footsteps, slow and deliberate, echoing from the shadows beyond the room. I froze, my blood turning to ice. I wasn't alone.

"Eliza," the voice came again, this time close—too close. It wasn't Derek's voice. This one was softer, almost sorrowful. It carried a weight, a depth that I couldn't place. "You've come so far."

I turned quickly, my heart leaping into my throat.

Standing in the doorway was a figure—tall, shadowed, and barely visible in the dim light. But there was something in the way the figure stood, the way the shadows clung to it, that told me everything I needed to know. I had seen this figure before. I had seen it in my dreams.

"Who are you?" I demanded, my voice shaky but defiant. The book in my hands felt heavier now, as though it were filled with more than just paper.

The figure stepped forward, the shadows shifting to reveal a face—a face I would never forget.

It was me.

But not exactly. The eyes were the same, but the expression was different—cold, distant, as though the person standing before me had forgotten who they were, or who they had been.

"I am what you've become," the figure said, its voice now laced with sorrow. "I am the part of you that you tried to forget."

The world around me seemed to narrow, the space contracting with the weight of those words. I couldn't breathe. I couldn't think. This—this thing was me, wasn't it? Some twisted reflection of who I was, or who I would become if I stayed here too long.

"You've been running from the truth," the figure continued, its voice a soft whisper now. "But you can't outrun yourself forever."

I stepped back, clutching the book to my chest, my mind whirling. There was no escaping this. No escaping what I had become.

The figure tilted its head, studying me with a look that seemed almost... pitying. "You have to face it, Eliza. You are the heart of the labyrinth."

The words struck me like a blow, and I staggered backward, the room spinning around me.

The door was still there, behind the figure, but it felt so far away now—too far.

And in that moment, I realized the truth: the labyrinth had never been about finding a way out. It had been about confronting what lay within.

18

The Veil Between Worlds

The air was heavy with an unseen tension, as if the very atmosphere itself was holding its breath. I couldn't move. The figure—my reflection, my shadow, my other—stood before me, its presence suffocating the space. The shadows around it clung, twisting in unnatural ways, as though they were extensions of the figure itself. Its eyes—my eyes—bore into me with a kind of knowing, a coldness that made my skin crawl.

"You can't outrun what you've become, Eliza," it whispered again, the voice a dark echo of my own. "You can only face it."

I stepped back, my heart hammering in my chest, every instinct screaming to run, to escape this place, this nightmare. But where would I run to? The labyrinth was not just a physical space—it was a prison of the mind. And now, I was face-to-face with the very thing I had been running from all this time: myself.

"What do you want from me?" My voice was barely a whisper,

but it seemed to resonate in the stillness, bouncing off the distant walls of the vast, empty room.

The figure didn't respond right away. It just stared at me, its gaze so intense that it felt like it was peeling back the layers of my soul, exposing every secret, every weakness. My hands trembled as I gripped the book tighter, the weight of it grounding me in this moment, even though everything inside me screamed to escape.

"You've been running for so long," the figure finally said, its voice soft, almost gentle now. "From the truth, from the choices you made. But the truth is here. It always has been."

I wanted to scream, to lash out at this thing that was not a thing at all, but a part of me, a part I had locked away for so long. I wanted to deny it, to tell it that it was wrong, that it was all just some twisted illusion conjured by the labyrinth. But deep down, I knew it was right. The truth had always been here, buried beneath the surface of my mind, waiting for me to confront it.

"I don't—" I began, but the figure cut me off, its voice growing more insistent.

"You don't want to accept it? You don't want to acknowledge what you've done?" The figure stepped closer, its movement slow and deliberate. "You promised yourself that you'd forget. That you'd walk away from everything you were. But you couldn't. Because it was never just about forgetting, Eliza. It was about embracing who you really are."

The words hit me like a punch to the gut. I staggered back, my breath coming in shallow gasps. My mind reeled, struggling to make sense of the flood of emotions crashing over me. The labyrinth, the book, this... this thing—it was all part of the same truth. And the truth was that I had never really escaped. I had only been running in circles, pretending that I could erase the past, that I could erase him—the man whose memory I had buried so deep inside me.

But the truth had a way of clawing its way to the surface, no matter how much I tried to ignore it. The truth was standing in front of me now, looking at me with eyes that were both mine and not mine. A mirror reflecting everything I had tried to outrun.

"You were never meant to be free," the figure said, its voice low, almost mournful now. "Not from this. Not from him."

I felt a sharp, jarring pain in my chest, a tightness that made it hard to breathe. My hands were trembling, my knees weak beneath me, but I couldn't look away from the figure. It was right. It had to be. Everything I had tried to forget, every part of me I had shoved into the deepest recesses of my mind, was now demanding to be acknowledged.

"Why did you leave him?" The figure's voice cut through the silence, its words like daggers in my heart. "Why did you break your promise to him? To us?"

The words hit with brutal force, and suddenly, I was no longer standing in that vast, empty room. I was back there—back in that place, that time—standing at the edge of the decision I had made all those years ago.

It was a dark night. The air had been thick with tension, heavy with unspoken words. Derek had been there, just like always, his face a mask of quiet intensity. But there had been something else in his eyes that night—something desperate, something that spoke of finality. The promise we had made, the bond we had shared, was now at the breaking point.

"Eliza," he had said, his voice barely above a whisper. "You don't have to do this. We can still make it through. We just have to—"

"I can't," I had interrupted, my voice cold, even though my heart was breaking. "I can't stay here. I can't keep pretending that everything will be okay. We're too different, Derek. We always were."

The look in his eyes had been one of devastation, but also of understanding. It was the same look he had given me just before I walked away—before I turned my back on everything we had, everything we could have been. The look of a man who knew he was losing me, but who could never truly make me stay.

"I can't keep living in this lie," I had said, my voice breaking with the weight of the words.

And then I had left. Left him behind. Left everything behind.

The memory crashed over me like a tidal wave, pulling me under, drowning me in guilt and regret. I had abandoned him. I had promised to forget him, to sever the bond we had, because I couldn't bear the thought of being tied to him forever. But in doing so, I had tied myself to the labyrinth instead. To the darkness. To the never-ending chase.

I snapped back to the present, gasping for air, the pain in my chest almost unbearable. The figure was still there, watching me, waiting for me to understand.

"You can't outrun it," it repeated, its voice colder now. "You've never been able to. Because you're still running from yourself."

I shook my head, my mind spinning. I couldn't breathe, couldn't think. This—this was the moment I had been dreading. The moment where I had to face the truth of my own choices, my own weakness.

The labyrinth had been my punishment. My penance for abandoning the one person who had mattered most in my life. And now, I was trapped. Trapped in the very web I had woven for myself.

The figure stepped closer, its form solidifying in the dim light. "You have to make a choice, Eliza," it said, its voice now full of finality. "You can leave this place. You can escape. But you have to accept what you've done. You have to face the cost of your decision."

My hands were shaking, the book slipping from my fingers as I collapsed to my knees. I couldn't breathe, couldn't think. The labyrinth, the figure, the memory of Derek—it was all closing in on me, suffocating me with its weight.

But somewhere, deep within me, a flicker of defiance sparked.

I would not be consumed by this. I would not let my past define me any longer. I would face it. I would face him.

I stood up slowly, my legs trembling beneath me, and I faced the figure—my reflection. This time, I didn't look away.

"I choose to remember," I said, my voice firm despite the fear gnawing at my insides. "I choose to face what I've done. And I choose to make it right."

The figure's eyes narrowed, a flicker of something—regret, or perhaps something darker—passing through them.

"Then go," it whispered, the shadows around it twisting, dissolving into the air. "But know this: you can never undo what you've done. You can only move forward."

The room around me began to fade, the shadows receding, the labyrinth's walls stretching back into the distance. And as the last of the darkness disappeared, I felt the weight lift from my shoulders. The way forward was clear.

But the journey wasn't over. The true challenge had just begun.

19

Echoes of the Unspoken

The silence in the room was suffocating. It clung to me like a second skin, pressing against my chest, making it hard to breathe. The shadows, though no longer as thick and oppressive as before, still lingered in the corners of the vast, empty space, as if waiting for something. Or someone.

I wasn't sure how long I had been standing there, my legs numb from kneeling on the cold, smooth floor. The figure—my reflection—had faded into the shadows, its last words echoing in my mind like a bitter wind. You can never undo what you've done. You can only move forward.

Forward. The word repeated itself in my head, each time feeling like a weight, a challenge, a reminder that the past was gone, and I was the one left to pick up the pieces. I had made my choice. I had faced the truth. But that didn't make what I had to do next any easier.

The labyrinth no longer felt like a maze of walls and corridors.

It felt like a vast expanse, stretching out before me in every direction, open and yet somehow closed. The book in my hands had changed again. The once-blank pages now filled with shifting symbols, lines and shapes that twisted and turned, their meaning hidden from view, but there was something about them—something familiar.

I glanced around, but the room remained unchanged. The door—the one through which I had entered—was still there, standing silently in the distance, like a forgotten relic of another time. I had to move. There was no choice. I could feel it in my bones. The labyrinth was no longer going to show me the way. I had to find it for myself.

I took a slow, hesitant step forward, my breath coming in sharp, shallow bursts as I walked. The air around me seemed to shift, cool against my skin, but the book in my hands grew heavier, as though urging me onward. Every step felt like it carried the weight of a hundred unspoken words, a hundred lost memories.

And then I heard it.

A soft sound at first, like a whisper carried on the wind. But it wasn't the wind. It was a voice. Familiar. Cold.

"Eliza."

I froze. My heart skipped a beat, and I instinctively gripped the book tighter, feeling the old leather crack under my fingertips. The voice came again, louder this time, cutting through the stillness like a blade.

"Eliza..."

I spun around, every muscle in my body locked in tension, my eyes searching the shadows, my breath caught in my throat. But there was nothing there—no figure, no reflection, just the empty space, stretching out before me, taunting me with its silence.

It had to be a trick. Another illusion, another game. But the voice—that voice—was too real. Too familiar.

"Derek?" I whispered, the name slipping from my lips before I could stop it.

For a moment, nothing happened. The room remained still, the shadows unmoving. But then, from the corner of my eye, I saw it. A figure. Tall. Dark. Standing just at the edge of the room, barely visible in the dim light. The outline of a man.

I couldn't breathe. My legs felt like they were made of stone as I stepped forward, inching closer, my heart pounding in my chest.

"Derek?" I called again, my voice a mix of hope and fear.

The figure didn't move, but the whisper came again, carried on the still air, this time louder, sharper, more urgent.

"Eliza..."

I reached for the figure, my hand trembling, but as I got closer, the air seemed to grow colder, the shadows thickening around me. It was like trying to walk through fog, the space narrowing with every step. My fingers brushed against something, but when I looked, it was empty.

The figure was gone.

But the voice remained.

I spun around, panic rising in my chest. The labyrinth was playing with me again. It was toying with my mind, pulling at the fragments of memory and fear that I had buried deep inside. You can never undo what you've done. You can only move forward.

I shut my eyes, pushing the voice out of my mind, forcing myself to focus. I had faced it before. I had faced him. But this—this was different. This wasn't just Derek's ghost. It was something more. Something darker.

"Enough," I whispered fiercely to the room, to the shadows, to the voice that still clung to the air. "I'm not afraid of you."

The silence that followed was deafening. The shadows seemed to recede, almost as though they had heard my words. But then, in the quiet, there came another sound—one I wasn't expecting.

Footsteps. Slow. Steady.

They echoed through the labyrinth, but this time, they weren't the quiet, unseen steps I had heard before. These were real, solid, with weight and purpose behind them. The sound of someone approaching.

I turned sharply, my pulse racing. But there was nothing.

Nothing but the faint glow of the symbols on the floor, their twisting shapes now glowing brighter, pulsing with an unnatural rhythm. I could feel the pull of them, the draw of their strange power.

And then I saw it.

The door.

But this time, it was different. This time, the door was wide open. And standing in the doorway was a figure—tall, cloaked in shadow, its features hidden in the dim light.

"You're not ready," a voice spoke from the figure, deep and resonant.

I couldn't speak. I couldn't move. The words felt like chains, holding me in place.

"You think you've faced the worst of it," the voice continued, stepping into the room, "but you're only at the beginning."

A chill ran down my spine. The shadows seemed to close in, tightening around me like a noose. I could feel the weight of the figure's presence, the gravity of its power, pressing in from all sides.

"You think you're free," it said again, its voice soft but somehow terrifying, "but there are parts of you—dark parts—that you've never confronted."

I opened my mouth to protest, to tell it that I had already faced the truth, that I had made my choice. But no sound came. My throat was dry, constricted, as though the very air had been stolen from my lungs.

The figure took another step forward, its form becoming clearer, more defined. It wasn't Derek. It wasn't my reflection. But it was something else—something I couldn't quite place.

And then, just as suddenly as it had appeared, the figure vanished, leaving me standing alone in the darkened room, surrounded by the swirling shadows of the labyrinth.

The silence that followed was deafening, crushing in its weight. I felt the pull of the symbols beneath me, and without thinking, I bent down, touching one of them.

The instant my fingers made contact with the glowing shapes, the room shifted, distorting around me like a ripple in water. The air grew heavy, thick with a strange pressure, and the shadows stretched, twisting toward me.

For a moment, everything stopped. Time itself seemed to freeze.

And then, in the distance, I heard it.

A door creaking open.

Another step closer. Another layer of the labyrinth peeled away.

And as I turned toward the sound, I knew without a doubt that nothing would ever be the same again.

20

The Pulse of the Abyss

The air felt thick, charged with something ancient and pulsing. I couldn't explain it, but the very walls of the labyrinth seemed to breathe, as if they were alive—like they were listening, waiting for me to make a move. Every step I took felt heavier, as though the ground itself was pushing against me, testing my resolve. I could feel it now—the presence, the energy that had been following me for so long. It was growing stronger, more tangible, and I knew, deep in my gut, that whatever was coming next would change everything.

The hallway in front of me stretched into darkness, the shadows now thicker than they had ever been. They seemed to curl and writhe, as if they had a life of their own. The symbols that had once glowed on the floor were now faint, their eerie light flickering as though fighting against some unseen force. I wanted to turn back. I wanted to flee from this place, from this suffocating feeling that I was being watched—not by the walls, not by the shadows, but by something... something much darker.

I paused, my breath shallow, my heart racing. The whispering wind had stopped, the footsteps had vanished, but the sense of being hunted had only grown stronger. My fingers clenched around the book, its edges worn, its pages filled with cryptic markings that I still couldn't fully understand.

It was then that I heard it—a faint, rhythmic sound. At first, I thought it was my heartbeat, but it was too steady, too deliberate. It was coming from somewhere ahead. A pulse. A thrum. Like the very heartbeat of the labyrinth itself.

I took a cautious step forward, my legs stiff and reluctant, but the pull of the unknown was too strong to resist. The sound was growing louder now, a low, throbbing rhythm that resonated through my chest, matching the beat of my own heart. Each step I took seemed to draw me closer to it, the pulse reverberating through the air, through the ground, until it felt like the very earth beneath my feet was alive.

The shadows were thickening again, pressing in on me from all sides, swirling around like a storm. I couldn't see anything clearly, but I could feel it—an almost tangible pressure closing in. It was as if the labyrinth itself was aware of my presence and was holding its breath, waiting for me to make the next move. The pulse was louder now, faster, stronger.

I had no choice but to follow it. I had come this far. There was no turning back.

As I walked, the shadows began to shift and stretch, the darkness opening up like a wound in the air. I stumbled, catching myself against the wall, my mind racing with questions. What was this place? What had I gotten myself into? The air felt colder now, and I pulled my jacket tighter around me, trying to stave off the chill.

The pulse was nearly deafening now, pounding in my ears. It felt like the very walls of the labyrinth were vibrating in sync with it. It was so strong, so overwhelming, that it seemed to blur everything around me, until there was nothing but the sound and the darkness, swallowing me whole.

And then, just as suddenly as it had begun, the pulse stopped.

The silence was absolute, crushing. My heart thudded painfully in my chest as I stood frozen, trying to make sense of what had just happened. For a long moment, I didn't move. I couldn't.

But then, I heard it. A sound so soft, so distant, that I almost didn't catch it. A faint scraping. It came from just ahead, somewhere in the darkness.

I blinked, trying to adjust my eyes, but there was nothing. No figure. No sign of movement. Just an empty space, a cavernous room that stretched on forever. The air was thick with an almost suffocating weight. I could feel it—something was waiting. Something was watching.

And then I saw it.

At the far end of the room, barely visible in the dim light, was a door. Or what I thought was a door. It wasn't like any door I had ever seen. It was carved into the stone, the edges jagged and uneven, as if it had been there for centuries, waiting for someone to open it.

I knew I had to go through it. The pulse—the strange, rhythmic beating—was coming from the other side. It was calling me. I had no choice but to approach it. My feet moved forward, slow, cautious, as if the very act of walking would somehow alert the shadows, bring them back to life.

I reached the door, my fingers brushing against the rough stone, the carvings strange and unfamiliar under my touch. There were symbols here, too, much like the ones in the hallway. They were intricate, almost hypnotic in their patterns. I could feel the pull of them, the weight of their significance. But as I traced one of the markings, something strange happened.

The door shuddered, a low, grinding sound coming from deep within its stone frame. The pulse that had been so steady before now quickened, faster, harder, almost erratic. It was as if the door itself was alive, reacting to my touch.

I stepped back, startled, but the door began to open on its own, the stone grinding against stone, screeching in protest. A dark, swirling light poured from the gap, too bright to look at directly, but too mesmerizing to ignore. The air felt charged with an energy I couldn't explain, a force that seemed to fill the space, pulsing, shifting, alive.

The moment the door was fully open, I stepped forward, compelled by the force, by the need to know what was on the other side. But as I crossed the threshold, the world seemed to tilt, the floor buckling beneath me. My breath caught in my throat as the shadows closed in around me, the pulse now deafening, a steady thrum that felt like it was coming from within my very bones.

And then, I saw it.

In the center of the room was a pool of black water, its surface smooth and still. The pulse was coming from there, I realized. From the water itself. There was no source, no visible cause for the sound—it was as if the water itself was alive, beating in time with some ancient rhythm.

I moved toward it, drawn by an invisible force. The water was black, so dark that it seemed to swallow the light, and as I gazed into its depths, I saw... something. A flicker of movement, a shadow that wasn't mine. A figure, indistinct, its features obscured by the darkness, but somehow, I knew it was waiting for me.

A whisper, a voice—a familiar voice—slipped into my mind.

"Eliza..."

My heart stopped.

I took a step back, my breath coming in sharp gasps, but my feet wouldn't obey. I couldn't move. My eyes were fixed on the pool, the dark water swirling, rippling, reacting to my gaze.

"You've come far..." The voice was clearer now, as though the very water itself was speaking. "But you have only begun to understand."

I reached out, trembling, my fingers just inches from the surface of the water. The pulse grew louder, faster, as if it were in sync with my heartbeat, each thump vibrating through the air, through my body.

And then the water began to ripple.

And the darkness closed in.

I wasn't sure if I was ready for what lay beneath the surface.

But there was no turning back.

21

Beneath the Surface

The water in front of me moved in a slow, deliberate dance, its surface shifting and swirling like a living thing. My fingers, still hovering just above the black, smooth sheen, ached with a strange, magnetic pull. I knew I had to touch it, but fear anchored me in place. I couldn't shake the feeling that the water wasn't just water—there was something more beneath it. Something hidden. Waiting.

I swallowed, my throat dry, the pulse in my chest quickening to match the rhythm of the water. The voice—the voice from the depths—echoed in my mind again, its words like a whispering promise, an invitation to something unknown, something that I wasn't sure I was ready for.

"You've come far... but the truth you seek lies beneath the surface."

The words felt like a weight, pressing on my chest, urging me to surrender, to let go of the fear that still gripped me. But deep down, I knew that whatever I uncovered in the depths would change everything. The water was a mirror to something I had yet to understand, something far beyond the labyrinth itself.

I took a shaky step forward, the sound of my boots muffled by the thick air. Each movement felt deliberate, as if I were being drawn into a current stronger than I could resist. The ripples on the surface of the water grew more intense, reacting to my presence, as if the very act of stepping closer was causing it to stir, to wake from its slumber.

Was it alive?

The thought flickered in my mind, a fleeting question that I couldn't ignore. But the answers didn't come. Only more ripples. More shadows beneath the surface.

I reached out slowly, my fingertips grazing the water. The moment my skin made contact, an electric jolt shot through me, a cold shock that traveled up my arm and into my chest, making my heart skip. The ripples spread out from the point of contact, distorting the surface, twisting it in impossible shapes.

And then, without warning, the surface shattered.

A sudden burst of movement, a crack that echoed through the air like thunder, and the water splashed violently against the edges of the pool. I staggered back, my pulse roaring in my ears as the world seemed to tilt, the ground beneath me trembling, as though the very fabric of reality was tearing apart.

I gripped the edge of the stone basin, my knuckles white with the effort of holding on, my eyes wide with panic. The water had become dark, churning, thick with shadows that seemed to writhe and twist beneath the surface. And then, through the darkness, I saw it.

A figure.

It emerged slowly, rising from the depths like a phantom summoned from some forgotten realm. A silhouette, tall and impossibly slender, its form shrouded in shadow, only the faintest hint of its features visible in the dim light. It didn't move like a human; it moved like something that wasn't bound by the same laws of nature. Its presence felt wrong, like a distortion of something pure.

The air around me grew colder, the temperature dropping so quickly that I could see my breath in the air. The figure's form grew clearer with each passing second, its features becoming sharper, more defined, until I could see its eyes—pale, haunting, filled with a cold emptiness that sent a chill through my very soul.

And then it spoke.

"You think you've come for answers, Eliza?"

The voice was low, hollow, like a distant echo from the past. It resonated deep in my chest, vibrating the very air around us.

"You think you've faced the darkness, but what you see before you is nothing compared to what you will find. The truth... is far darker than you can imagine."

I recoiled, my breath catching in my throat, my hand instinctively pulling back from the water. The figure's gaze followed me, unblinking, as though it could see straight through me, into the very core of my being.

The air around me felt heavy, oppressive, as though the weight of the figure's presence was closing in on me from all sides. My heart pounded in my chest, and I felt my legs grow weak beneath me.

"I—" I choked, trying to form a sentence, but the words were caught in my throat. The weight of the figure's gaze was suffocating, its silence unbearable.

"You are so close, Eliza," it said, its voice softer now, almost coaxing. "So close to the truth, but you don't understand. You haven't seen everything."

I shook my head, my pulse racing. I didn't understand. I didn't know what it wanted from me, but I couldn't stop myself from asking the question.

"What is this?" My voice cracked, the words trembling as I spoke. "What do you want from me?"

The figure's lips curled into a smile, but it wasn't a smile of comfort or reassurance. It was the smile of something older, something far more ancient than anything I had encountered in the labyrinth.

"What I want from you... is simple," it whispered, its voice a cold breath against my skin. "I want you to understand that you are nothing but a part of this. A part of the darkness that you fear. You cannot escape it. It will consume you, Eliza. And you will become just like me."

I felt a chill crawl up my spine, a wave of dread crashing over me, paralyzing me with fear. Like me? I thought. What did that mean?

The figure stretched its hand toward me, its fingers long and delicate, its skin pale and slick, as though it were made of something more than flesh. The pulse from the water grew louder, almost deafening now, as though it were beckoning me forward, pulling me into the depths with the figure.

"You don't understand yet," it said again, its eyes burning with an unsettling intensity. "But you will. When you open your eyes to the truth, when you see what lies beneath it all, you will know. You will know exactly what I mean."

I took a step back, my heart hammering in my chest as the figure's hand reached closer, its fingers brushing against the edge of the stone basin. And for the briefest of moments, I saw it—a glimmer of something ancient in its eyes, something that spoke to me, deep within my soul. It was the truth. The one I had been running from.

"You—" I gasped, taking another step back, "You're not real!"

But the figure only laughed, a sound like dry leaves scraping against stone.

"I'm more real than you can comprehend," it replied, its voice low and resonant. "You are the one who's not real, Eliza. You've been living in a lie, running from something you can't escape. The truth is here. Right in front of you. All you have to do is open your eyes."

I stumbled back further, my feet slipping on the stone, my breath coming in sharp, ragged gasps. The pulse was deafening now, the shadows closing in around me like a tightening noose. The figure's smile twisted, its eyes glowing with an eerie light, and the water began to churn violently again, as if something was about to emerge—something that would be far worse than the figure before me.

And then, with a final, horrifying scream, the figure lunged.

But as it reached for me, everything went black.

I awoke with a gasp, heart racing, the world spinning around me. The darkness was all-encompassing. Cold. Distant.

But something else was there.

A sound. A whisper.

"Welcome to the abyss, Eliza."

And I realized, with a sinking feeling in my gut, that I was no longer alone.

22

The Weight of Silence

I awoke in complete darkness. My body felt like it was sinking into the cold ground beneath me, but there was no floor to feel, no tangible surface beneath my hands. It was as though I had been swallowed whole by the void, and the weight of it pressed against my chest, making it hard to breathe.

Panic surged in my veins, but I swallowed it back, forcing myself to stay still. My heart pounded, loud and erratic in the silence that enveloped me. The air smelled musty, thick with the scent of decay, as though I had been buried alive. My fingers brushed the floor—smooth, slick stone. But even though I was certain of my position, the sensation of not being able to see anything, of being utterly blind, made my mind race.

"Where am I?" The words came out in a whisper, a shaky breath escaping my lips. No answer. Only the sound of my own voice, swallowed up by the oppressive darkness.

I pushed myself to sit up, my legs feeling weak beneath me,

as though they hadn't borne weight in too long. My hands trembled as they met the stone again, searching for something, anything that could anchor me, something familiar in this alien world.

My mind was still caught on the figure. The haunting figure that had risen from the depths of the water. It had been so real. Its voice, its presence—everything about it had been undeniable. The way it spoke... "You will become just like me..." The words hung in the air, lingering like a shadow I couldn't shake off. And now, I had awoken in this void—this nothingness.

A noise cut through the stillness, a soft scraping sound, distant but growing louder with every passing second. It was like claws dragging across stone. My skin prickled, and I froze, listening intently. Was it the figure again? Had I somehow fallen into its world, its domain? The thought made the air feel even colder, more suffocating.

I dared not move, waiting for the sound to grow closer. It didn't take long. A faint breath—barely audible—touched the back of my neck. My pulse raced, and I whirled around, my body lurching instinctively to escape. But there was nothing. No figure, no presence.

Just... silence. Deep, oppressive silence.

I took a shallow breath and slowly let it out, my hands clenched in fists at my sides, nails digging into my palms. My mind raced for answers, but there was only one thought that kept pushing its way through the fear: It's not over. This isn't over.

"Eliza," came the voice again, far too close. It was a whisper, but it echoed in my mind like a command. My breath hitched in my throat, and I forced myself to stay still.

I looked down at my hands, trembling in the dark, realizing the weight of them. As though they had carried something far heavier than they should have. A flicker of memory stirred in the back of my mind, fragments of faces, voices, the weight of things unsaid.

The whispers grew louder, indistinct, layering on top of one another like a cacophony of voices lost in time. They seemed to surround me, coming from all directions, wrapping themselves around me like invisible chains, suffocating, strangling. I opened my mouth to scream, but the sound was swallowed before it even left my lips.

Suddenly, a light appeared, faint at first, like a flicker of hope in the distance. It was dim, yet it grew stronger as I blinked, my eyes struggling to adjust to the change. The light seemed to move, shifting from one corner of the dark space to the other. Slowly, methodically, as if it had a purpose.

I reached out for it, desperate for some answer, something to explain the nightmare that had swallowed me. My legs felt unsteady as I rose to my feet, but I forced myself forward, my feet ungracefully stumbling over the uneven surface, every step echoing in the silence.

As I walked, the light flickered once more and then stabilized, revealing what lay beyond. A figure. Another one. Taller than the last. Its outline was obscured by the same eerie glow, but I could see enough to make out the shape—long, sharp, angular, like the outline of a creature that shouldn't exist.

This figure didn't speak at first. It just stood there, motionless, like a statue frozen in time. I wanted to turn and flee, to escape this new terror, but something kept me in place. Some pull, some force I couldn't understand.

Then it spoke. The voice was cold, hollow, the words cutting through the air like ice. "You've come too far, Eliza. And now you will understand."

The weight of those words landed heavy on my chest, like a stone sinking deeper into my lungs. I staggered back, my body slamming into the cold stone wall behind me, the sudden shock making my teeth rattle.

"Understand what?" I gasped, my voice shaking with the force of my fear. "What do you want from me?"

The figure stepped closer, its outline still distorted by the strange glow, but with each step, it became clearer, more defined. I could see the way its arms—too long, too thin—hung at its sides. The skin was pale, almost translucent, as if it had been drained of life, of color. And its eyes—those eyes—were a deep, black abyss, nothingness that seemed to devour all light.

"You are not the first to come here," it said, its voice like the rustle of dead leaves. "Not the first to search for answers.

But all who come here must pay the price. You think you are different, that you are exempt from the fate of the others who have come before you. But the truth is… there is no escaping."

I wanted to scream again, but the words died in my throat, trapped beneath the weight of its gaze. It was as though it could see every fear, every secret I had buried deep inside. Everything that had haunted me for so long. It saw through me.

"You think you are looking for truth, Eliza, but the truth will never set you free. Not in this place."

I recoiled, my chest tightening. I felt the panic welling up again, threatening to choke me, but I didn't move. I couldn't. My legs were like lead, frozen in place.

"Why?" I whispered, the word escaping before I could stop it. "Why me?"

The figure's lips twisted into a smile, but it was a smile devoid of warmth, devoid of anything human. "Because you are the one who was meant to uncover it. You are the one who has to face the truth… whether you want to or not."

A cold, hollow laugh echoed around me, and for a moment, I felt the ground beneath me shift, tremble. Like the very foundations of the place were crumbling.

And then, in a flash of blinding light, it was gone.

I stood in the darkness once more, alone, my body shaking,

my mind a tangled mess of fear and confusion. What had just happened? What had it meant? The words—the promises, the warnings—echoed in my mind.

But one thing was clear: I had just uncovered a deeper layer of this twisted puzzle. And the truth I had been seeking? It was far darker than I could have ever imagined.

23

The Shadows That Follow

The moment the light flickered out, I felt the air grow thicker, suffocating. The oppressive darkness returned with a vengeance, and every inch of space felt like it was closing in on me. I stood there in the quiet, my heart hammering, my mind racing to process what had just happened. The figure, its words, the cold laugh—it was all too surreal, too much to grasp in the fragile state I was in.

The world around me felt suspended, like time itself had frozen. I couldn't shake the feeling that I wasn't alone, that the presence of something—someone—was still lingering in the shadows, watching, waiting. It was as though the darkness was alive, and I was its prey.

I reached out, my hands trembling, and fumbled along the walls, seeking anything that could anchor me to reality. The stone beneath my fingers was rough, damp, like it had been here far longer than I could imagine. The faint scent of mildew clung to the air, mixing with the strange metallic tang that still lingered from the earlier encounter. Every sound felt amplified, too loud, like the silence itself was pressing in on me.

A noise broke the stillness—a soft shuffle, like something dragging across the ground, slow, deliberate. My breath caught in my throat, and I froze. It was closer this time, just beyond the edge of my vision. My heart thudded against my ribs, and my pulse quickened, every instinct in me telling me to move, to run. But my feet wouldn't budge. It was as if the shadows had rooted me in place, leaving me powerless.

The shuffling stopped.

I strained my ears, my senses heightened in the suffocating darkness. The silence stretched on, stretching into eternity, thick and heavy. I dared not make a sound, not a single movement, for fear that whatever waited in the dark would hear me. My breath was shallow, my chest tight, the weight of the moment pressing on me from all sides.

Then, just as I thought I might lose my sanity to the silence, I heard a voice. Soft, whispering, like a breath against my ear.

"Eliza..."

I gasped, the name echoing in my mind, reverberating through every inch of my being. The voice was familiar, but twisted—familiar, but wrong. It sent a shiver down my spine, and I turned my head, straining to see through the impenetrable dark, but there was nothing. No figure, no presence. Just emptiness.

"You cannot hide from me."

The voice came again, closer this time. It was colder now, sharper, a serpent's hiss that slithered through my veins. I jerked back, my hands shooting out to find something, anything, to keep me steady. My fingertips brushed against the cold stone wall, and I tried to steady myself. My breathing was ragged, my pulse a drumbeat in my ears.

I closed my eyes for a split second, trying to steady myself, to think through the panic threatening to overwhelm me. I had to calm down. I had to make sense of this. But the more I tried to focus, the more the shadows seemed to crowd in on me, pressing closer. The weight of them was unbearable, suffocating. It was like the darkness itself was alive, swirling around me, pulling at my skin.

And then, it happened.

A hand—ice-cold, impossibly cold—brushed against my shoulder. The sensation was sharp, as though something not quite human had touched me, its fingers grazing my skin with a chill that made my blood run cold. I whipped around, but there was nothing there.

The air was too still, too quiet. My breath was loud in my ears, and I could feel the pounding of my heart like it was about to break free from my chest. I didn't dare to speak, not after the whispers. I didn't want to hear that voice again. But the silence was unbearable. The walls were closing in, the weight of the unknown pressing harder, suffocating me with its cold embrace.

A scraping sound—this time louder, closer. The same sound from before, like claws dragging across the stone. It was unmistakable now. Something was there, something was moving in the dark, just beyond the edge of my vision. My fingers curled into fists, nails digging into my palms as I fought to remain still, to listen, to understand what was happening.

The scraping stopped.

The silence returned, but it was different now. Heavier. Thicker. It felt like something was lurking just behind me, its presence so close that I could almost feel it breathing down my neck. Every instinct screamed at me to run, but I couldn't move. The fear held me in place like a vice, squeezing the breath out of me.

"I know you're there," I whispered into the darkness, my voice shaking. I wanted to sound braver than I felt, but the words barely escaped my lips.

For a moment, there was nothing.

Then, a soft chuckle. It was low, menacing, and it sent a wave of terror through me, making my skin crawl.

"You can't run from your past, Eliza," the voice purred, its tone dripping with malice. "You can't escape what you've done."

I shuddered, the words hitting me like a physical blow. What did it mean? What was it talking about? What had I done? The question reverberated in my mind, but I couldn't find the answers. Not here. Not in the suffocating dark.

My fingers found the cold stone once more, desperately searching for something, anything, that could give me a way out. But the darkness seemed endless. No light. No escape.

"Who are you?" My voice was barely a whisper, but I could feel the weight of it, the question that had been gnawing at me ever since I had first woken in this cursed place. "What do you want from me?"

The laughter rose again, louder this time, filling the air with an unnerving sense of satisfaction, as if my fear fed it. It was the only thing that filled the space now, its echoes bouncing off the walls, growing, growing, until it seemed to stretch into eternity.

"You already know the answer," it said, and the words wrapped around me like chains, dragging me into the depths of the unknown. "You know why you're here. You know why you can't leave."

And then, just as suddenly as it had come, the laughter stopped.

The silence returned.

But this time, it was different.

This time, I could hear something else beneath it.

A faint sound. A faint thump.

Like footsteps.

24

The Heart Beneath the Stone

I didn't dare breathe. The thump echoed through the air, low and deliberate, like someone—or something—was taking careful, measured steps. It was faint, but unmistakable. Each thud was a whisper of impending danger, a promise of something dark and unyielding. I couldn't see anything, couldn't hear anything beyond that rhythmic beat in the silence. But I knew, deep in my bones, that I wasn't alone.

I strained my ears, trying to pinpoint the source of the sound, but the darkness had swallowed it all. The air felt heavier now, almost suffocating, and the walls around me seemed to pulse with a life of their own, as though the very stone was aware of my every move. Every inch of my skin crawled, but my feet remained rooted to the ground, my legs frozen in place by a mixture of fear and uncertainty.

The thumping continued, growing louder, closer, until it was so deafening that it drowned out everything else. I clenched my fists, nails biting into my palms, my breath shallow and quick. I had to do something, had to make sense of this, but I couldn't move. Not while that sound was getting closer, and closer still.

Then, suddenly, the thumping stopped.

A chill ran through me, colder than the air, colder than anything I had ever felt before. The kind of cold that makes your blood run thick, like you're drowning in ice. The silence that followed was even worse than the sound itself. It was the kind of silence that wraps around you, presses against your chest, suffocates you slowly. It felt like something was waiting. Watching.

I took a deep, unsteady breath, forcing my body to move. My legs screamed in protest as I forced myself to take a step, then another, and another, each one feeling like a battle against the unseen force holding me in place. The stone beneath my feet felt sharp and uneven, as if it was intentionally trying to trip me, to make me falter.

But I couldn't stop. I couldn't stay here. Not while the silence stretched on, thick and heavy, pressing against me.

And then, as if in response to my determination, a low growl pierced the quiet—a growl that seemed to come from every direction at once. The sound made my blood freeze. It was deep and guttural, like the growl of some monstrous beast, and it vibrated through my very bones.

I stumbled back, my hands flying to the wall for support, my heart racing faster than I thought possible.

"Who's there?" My voice came out as a whisper, barely more than a breath, but it seemed to fill the space. The silence swallowed it whole.

No answer.

But I wasn't alone.

I could feel it now. The weight of something in the room, just beyond my reach. I could hear its breath, slow and labored, as though it was waiting for something. Waiting for me.

A shuffle.

Another step.

Then, without warning, the light flickered on.

For a split second, everything was too bright. The sudden shift from darkness to light made my vision swim, and I squinted, blinking furiously to adjust. But as my eyes refocused, I saw it.

A figure.

A woman—or what had once been a woman—stood before me, her face hidden in shadows, her body cloaked in tattered rags that clung to her form like a second skin. Her eyes, though, were unmistakable. They were the darkest shade of black, so deep they seemed to swallow the light. They stared at me with a hunger that chilled me to the core, a predatory gleam that sent a tremor through my very soul.

Her lips parted in a slow, deliberate smile, but it wasn't a smile of kindness. It was twisted, cruel, full of malice, as if every part of her being existed only to cause pain.

And yet, beneath that smile, there was something else. A flicker of recognition. A flash of something I couldn't place. Something that felt—familiar.

"Eliza..." Her voice was smooth and cold, like ice, but there was an edge to it. A tremor of something raw. Something desperate.

I didn't know what to say. What could I say? My mind raced, my thoughts scattered like leaves in the wind. The name... she knew my name. But how? Why?

"You've been running for so long," she continued, her voice low and mocking. "You think you can hide from the truth? You think you can bury it beneath the stone?"

The stone. The same stone that had been my prison. The stone that had been here long before I ever set foot in this place.

My eyes darted around the room, trying to find an escape, something—anything—that could offer me a way out. But the walls were closing in, and the woman's presence was suffocating. She was too close now, standing just a few feet away, her eyes locked on mine, her smile never faltering.

I tried to speak, but my throat was dry, choked with fear. I opened my mouth, but the words caught in my chest.

"You've forgotten so much," she said, her voice thick with regret. "But you can't forget forever. The past always catches up with you, Eliza. Always."

I shook my head, confusion clouding my mind. "I don't... I don't know you."

She laughed, a bitter, broken sound that echoed off the stone walls, reverberating through my very being. "You don't remember, do you? How could you? How could you ever forget what you've done?"

I staggered backward, my breath coming in short, panicked gasps. What was she talking about? What had I done? What was this woman? She seemed to know so much—too much. My mind reeled, trying to piece together fragments, trying to make sense of the chaos, but the pieces wouldn't fit.

"You buried it," she said, stepping closer now, her eyes dark pools of infinite depth. "But you can't hide forever. You can't bury the truth. It always comes back."

The air grew colder still, and I could feel the weight of her words pressing down on me, crushing me under their gravity. My knees buckled beneath me, and I sank to the ground, my hands trembling as they pressed against the cold stone floor.

"The heart beneath the stone," she whispered, bending down so that her face was inches from mine, her breath hot and rancid. "It's still beating, Eliza. And it always will."

The words echoed in my mind as the darkness rushed in again, swallowing the light. And I was left with nothing but the sound of a heart, beating, beating, beating—beneath the stone.

25

Beneath the Veil of Memory

I didn't move. Not even when the chill in the air seemed to wrap itself tighter around my chest, squeezing the breath from my lungs. The stone beneath me felt cold and unforgiving, pressing against my back like a grave that had waited far too long for its occupant. My hands trembled as I clutched them together, trying to still the frantic beat of my heart. But nothing, nothing could quell the terror that had clawed its way into my very bones.

The woman... the thing that had once been a woman... stood a few paces away, her dark eyes still boring into mine. Every word she spoke seemed to etch itself into the very fabric of my being, carving deep into places I thought I had long buried.

"You think you're free," she murmured, her voice like the scrape of metal against stone, "but you're not. Not while the past still has its grip on you."

I swallowed hard, trying to steady my breath. The words

swirled in my mind, threatening to drown me in the heavy fog of confusion. What past? What was she talking about? I had no memory of her, none at all, but there was something—something in the back of my mind—that felt almost familiar about her presence. It was as though she'd always been there, waiting in the shadows, lurking just out of reach.

"I don't know you," I whispered, the words barely leaving my throat. "I don't know anything anymore."

The woman smiled, but it wasn't a comforting smile. It wasn't a smile at all. It was more like a grimace, a twisted parody of something that could have once been human. "You don't remember, do you?" she asked softly, her voice thick with mockery. "You've forgotten the truth, buried it beneath the veil of memory. But it's always there, Eliza. Always waiting for you to remember."

My hands clenched into fists, my nails digging into the palms of my hands. I felt the heat of panic rising in my chest, but I couldn't move. I couldn't even make myself scream. I just... stared at her, my mind racing to make sense of it all.

"Who are you?" I forced the words out, my voice shaking with desperation. "What do you want from me?"

Her smile widened, her eyes narrowing into slits. "What I want is irrelevant, Eliza. What matters is what you're running from."

A sudden, sharp pain shot through my head, a piercing throb that made my vision blur. I gasped, my hand flying to my forehead, but the pain didn't relent. It was like something was clawing at my mind, tearing through the layers of memory, trying to break free.

"Stop!" I screamed, my voice raw and desperate. "Please... I can't take it anymore! What do you want from me?"

But the woman just stood there, unmoving, her dark eyes locked onto mine. Her lips barely moved as she spoke again, her words cutting through the chaos in my mind.

"You think you can escape it, Eliza. But you can't. You're bound to the past. Bound to the stone that holds your truth."

The pain in my head intensified, blurring everything around me. My breath came in ragged gasps, and I felt the floor beneath me start to tilt, as if the very room was shifting, rearranging itself into a nightmare. I squeezed my eyes shut, trying to block out the images that danced behind my eyelids—flashes of memories that I couldn't hold onto, faces I couldn't name, places I had never been.

"I don't remember," I whispered, my voice breaking. "I can't remember anything..."

The woman's expression softened for the briefest moment, but there was no warmth in it. Only pity. "That's the tragedy of it all, Eliza. You've forgotten because you don't want to face what you've done. But you will remember. You have no choice."

I shook my head violently, trying to shake the thoughts from my mind, trying to push the pain away, but it was no use. I could feel it. The truth. It was just out of reach, hidden beneath the surface of my fractured mind, waiting to break free.

Suddenly, the air around me seemed to change. The oppressive weight that had been bearing down on me lifted, just for a moment. And in that moment, a whisper of clarity broke through the fog.

The stone. She had said something about the stone.

I opened my eyes, the room now dimmer, the shadows crawling at the edges of my vision. The woman was still standing there, but I wasn't looking at her anymore. My eyes had drifted to the far corner of the room, where a faint light flickered. It wasn't much—just a small, almost imperceptible glow—but it was enough to draw me in. Enough to make me wonder if the stone she had spoken of was more than just a metaphor.

I rose unsteadily to my feet, my legs weak, trembling with each step. My body protested, but I pushed forward, driven by something that I couldn't fully understand. The flickering light grew brighter as I neared it, and the shadows seemed to part for me, clearing a path.

And then, I saw it.

A stone. Not just any stone, but a large, weathered slab of rock, half-buried in the dirt. Its surface was smooth, almost polished, despite the years of neglect. But it wasn't the stone itself that drew me in. It was what was carved into it.

Symbols. Strange, ancient symbols that seemed to pulse with energy, glowing faintly in the dim light. As I reached out to touch the stone, a shock of electricity jolted through my fingertips, making my body jerk back.

The woman's voice echoed from behind me, sharp and triumphant. "You've found it. You've found the truth."

I turned slowly, my heart pounding in my chest. "What is this?" I asked, my voice trembling with a mixture of fear and disbelief.

"The heart beneath the stone," she whispered, her eyes gleaming with a sinister light. "It's the key, Eliza. The key to everything."

My fingers brushed against the stone once more, and as they made contact, the symbols began to glow brighter. The ground beneath my feet trembled, and the room seemed to collapse in on itself. The truth—the truth that had been buried for so long—was finally emerging.

And I was no longer sure if I was ready to face it.

26

The Echoes of Forgotten Voices

I couldn't breathe. The air was thick, suffocating, swirling with a heaviness that made my chest ache. I tried to step back, to escape from the overwhelming sensation that was now consuming me, but my legs wouldn't move. It was as if the earth beneath me had fused with my body, anchoring me in place.

The stone was still glowing in front of me, its ancient symbols pulsing with an eerie, rhythmic light. Each pulse seemed to reverberate in my bones, like the beat of a drum calling me to some dark, forbidden place. I could hear it—the faint whisper of something, someone, behind the sound of my own heartbeat. It was as though the stone itself was speaking, its language older than anything I had ever known.

"You don't understand," a voice whispered, its tone like the rustling of dry leaves, barely audible yet unmistakably there. I turned toward it, my breath shallow, my heart racing. But there was no one—just shadows, stretching and twisting in the dim light.

I shook my head, trying to clear the fog that clouded my thoughts. "What is this?" I croaked, my voice sounding foreign, distant. "What do you want from me?"

The whispers grew louder, clearer, like a chorus of voices calling from the depths of the earth, from places I could never have imagined. They were urgent, frantic, full of desperation.

"You have to listen," one voice pleaded, its tone breaking like glass. "The truth is buried... buried under layers of lies, Eliza. You can't escape it. You can't outrun what you've done."

Another voice, this one cold and indifferent, followed. "She thinks she's free. But she's not. None of us are."

My hands clenched into fists, the raw edges of my nails digging into my palms. The stone. It was like a magnet, pulling me closer, forcing me to confront whatever it was that I had buried so deeply within myself. The voices were relentless now, each one intertwining with the others, creating a maddening symphony of accusations and half-remembered regrets.

"Why won't you remember?" the first voice whispered again, almost tenderly. "Why do you keep running from the truth?"

I pressed my hands to my ears, trying to block them out, but the voices only grew louder, more insistent. And then, just as quickly as they had started, they stopped.

The silence was deafening.

I stood in the quiet, my breath coming in ragged gasps, my pulse hammering in my throat. My mind raced, scrambling to make sense of everything that had just happened. What was real? What was a product of my fractured memory?

I slowly, cautiously, turned back toward the stone. The symbols on its surface were now glowing brighter, as if reacting to my presence. I reached out again, this time with purpose, my fingers brushing the cold stone's surface. The moment my skin made contact, the world seemed to shift around me.

The room blurred, as though reality itself was warping, bending to the will of the stone. And then, in an instant, everything froze.

I was no longer in the room.

I was somewhere else.

Somewhere dark, damp, and suffocating.

I was standing in the middle of a stone corridor, the walls lined with ancient carvings. The air was thick with the scent of mildew and decay, and the floor beneath my feet was slick with what I could only assume was moisture—dark, stagnant water that sloshed around my ankles with every step.

My breath quickened. The weight of the place pressed down on me, and I instinctively knew that this wasn't a place I was meant to be. It wasn't a place that anyone was meant to be. But my feet carried me forward anyway, as if they had a mind of their own. The whispering voices were back now, rising up from the shadows, their words unintelligible but undeniably urgent.

"Eliza…" The word cut through the darkness, a familiar name—my name—spoken in a voice that sent a chill down my spine.

I stopped. The hairs on the back of my neck stood on end as I turned in the direction of the voice. It was then that I saw her.

She stood at the end of the corridor, her figure shrouded in shadow. She was tall, unnaturally so, and her silhouette seemed to waver as though she were made of smoke, her features indistinct, blurred.

"Who are you?" I asked, my voice trembling.

The figure took a step forward, and with that movement, the shadows seemed to swallow her whole, leaving only the eerie sound of footsteps echoing off the stone walls.

I wanted to run. I wanted to scream, to turn and flee from this place, from this nightmare. But my legs were frozen, rooted to the spot.

"Eliza…" the voice called again, this time filled with unmistakable sorrow.

And then, with a suddenness that made me gasp, the figure

emerged from the darkness, stepping into the dim light. Her face was barely visible, but the faint glow that seemed to emanate from her was enough to see the sorrow etched into her features. Her eyes—those eyes—were wide, pleading, desperate.

It was then that I realized—this was a memory.

A memory I had tried to forget.

She stepped closer, her feet making no sound as they met the wet stone floor. "You remember now, don't you?" she asked softly, the words dripping with something like regret. "You remember what you did."

I staggered back, my hands shaking as they reached out to steady myself against the wall. The voices in my head were deafening now, their words a cacophony of rage and sorrow. And the woman—whoever she was—was still moving toward me, her expression unchanged, her eyes locked on mine.

"No..." I whispered, shaking my head. "I don't remember. I don't..."

But the woman's voice grew louder, more insistent. "You do. You remember everything, Eliza. You're the one who buried it. The one who buried me."

I gasped, my heart racing, as the truth began to claw its way to the surface. The memories I had hidden away—the memories I had tried to forget—were returning now, flooding my mind in a rush of images too sharp, too painful. The woman was not a stranger.

She was me.

And I was the one who had caused it all.

I was the one who had buried the truth.

27

The Unspoken Truth

The room spun. A dizzying swirl of shadows and light. My breath caught in my throat as I stood there, frozen in the dim glow of the stone. The woman's face—the face of someone I had buried deep in my past—stared back at me, her eyes dark and knowing, as though she had been waiting for this moment for years.

"You don't remember, do you?" she whispered, her voice low, almost tender. The air thickened, pressing in on me from all sides. My hands were clammy, my pulse racing, but I couldn't look away from her. I wanted to scream, to run, but my body refused to move. It was as if I were trapped in some twisted dream where the rules of reality didn't apply.

"No..." I said, the word escaping from my lips before I could stop it. "I don't understand. Who are you?"

Her smile—sad, knowing—flickered, and she took a step closer. The closer she came, the more her figure seemed to lose its solidity. She was almost... ethereal. Fading in and out, like a memory that couldn't quite hold on to the present. Her presence felt ancient, as if she had been a part of this place long before I ever set foot in it.

"You know who I am," she replied, her voice now carrying a trace of frustration. "You've always known, Eliza."

I stepped back, my mind a whirlwind of confusion and fear. My name. How did she know my name? How did she know anything about me?

"Stop." I held up a hand, my voice shaking with uncertainty. "Stop! I don't—"

But the woman wasn't listening. She continued moving closer, her steps soundless against the stone floor. "You were the one who sealed it away," she said. "You were the one who locked me in the dark, buried me in the past so deep that even you couldn't find me."

"No! I didn't do that," I gasped, my mind racing. "I don't—" But the words failed me, fading into the suffocating silence that filled the room.

Her eyes burned into mine, and in that moment, I felt a shiver run through me—cold, sharp, as though something inside me had been touched, something that had been dormant for years, waiting for the right moment to awaken.

"You did," she insisted, her voice now echoing through the

room. "You buried the truth because it was too painful to remember. Because it would destroy you to face it."

A cold knot of dread formed in my stomach. "What truth?" My voice trembled, but I could barely get the words out.

The woman's smile faded, replaced by something darker. She stepped forward again, and I could feel the weight of her gaze, the way it seemed to pierce through me, digging into places I didn't want to acknowledge.

"The truth about what happened that night," she said, her voice softer now, almost a whisper. "The night everything changed. The night I disappeared."

My heart skipped a beat. The night she disappeared. My mind grasped at the memory, but it was like trying to hold water in my hands—it slipped away, always out of reach. I had buried that night long ago. It was too painful, too raw. It was a wound I couldn't let myself reopen.

"No..." I whispered, shaking my head. "I don't... I don't remember. Please."

The woman stopped in front of me now, so close that I could almost feel the weight of her breath on my skin. Her eyes were wide, almost frantic.

"You remember," she said, her voice insistent. "You remember everything. Don't lie to yourself, Eliza. You know what you did."

I stumbled backward, my legs weak beneath me. I couldn't take it anymore—the pressure, the voices, the suffocating feeling that I was about to lose everything I thought I knew. The walls of the room seemed to close in, narrowing until the air felt as though it were being sucked out of my lungs.

I had to get out. I had to escape. But where could I go? The room, the stone, the woman—everything felt like a trap, a net closing in around me, tightening, pulling me toward the one thing I was most afraid of.

The truth.

"Eliza," she whispered again, her voice now a soft, aching plea. "Don't you remember? You were the last one to see me..."

I squeezed my eyes shut, the images from that night flooding into my mind in a torrent. My head spun, the pieces falling into place, but they didn't make sense. I remembered bits and pieces—fragments, flashes of faces, of a struggle. My breath hitched in my chest as something began to surface, something dark, something I wasn't ready to face.

"No..." I shook my head again, frantic now. "I didn't... I didn't do it. I didn't mean to..."

The woman's face softened for a moment, her expression one of sorrow. "You didn't mean to?" she asked, her voice barely a whisper. "You didn't mean to, but you did."

I recoiled as the truth hit me like a slap. The memories, the moments I had locked away for so long, were returning with brutal clarity. The fight. The argument. The way things had spiraled out of control. The guilt. The fear. The horror of knowing what had happened, even if I hadn't fully understood it until now.

But now, it was too late. The truth was here, looming before me like an insurmountable mountain. And I couldn't escape it anymore.

"You killed me," she said, her voice breaking, and for the first time, there was no trace of anger, only despair. "And now you have to live with it."

I stumbled backward, my mind reeling. The ground beneath me felt unstable, shifting, as if the world itself were crumbling away. I could feel the weight of her words in my chest, pressing down with the force of a thousand storms.

I opened my mouth to speak, but no sound came out.

And in that moment, the room—everything—fell away. The woman, the stone, the shadows—all of it vanished, swallowed by a darkness so complete, I couldn't even see my own hand in front of my face.

It was the kind of darkness that left you feeling lost, abandoned, like you were floating in an endless void. And yet, somewhere in that void, I knew that the woman's voice was still with me, whispering, echoing in the hollow space between my thoughts.

"You'll never escape it, Eliza. Never."

28

The Echoes of Silence

The silence in the room was suffocating. It pressed down on me like a heavy weight, suffocating any breath I might have taken. My heart pounded in my chest, a frantic rhythm that reverberated in my ears. I stood in the middle of the old, crumbling house—its walls now bare and haunting, stripped of the vibrant life they once held. The windows were shattered, the glass littering the floor like forgotten promises, but outside, there was nothing but darkness. Not a single star in the sky, not a glimmer of light to guide me.

I felt like I was suffocating in this place, suffocating in the truth I had just uncovered. I could still hear her words echoing in my mind, as if the very air had absorbed them and refused to let them go.

You killed me.

I shook my head, trying to push the words out of my mind. I wanted to scream, to tear at the walls, to run far, far away from here. But my feet wouldn't move. I was rooted to the spot, trapped in this house, trapped in my past. My hands trembled at my sides, and every instinct screamed at me to get out, to escape before it was too late.

But I couldn't escape. Not now.

You killed me.

Her voice haunted me, always lurking at the edge of my thoughts. It was so quiet, so persistent, it seemed to fill the entire room. The words echoed in the empty space like the sound of a clock ticking down to something inevitable—something I couldn't avoid.

I had to leave. I had to get out. But where would I go? There was no escape from the truth. The past had come rushing back like a flood, and there was no way to stop it. The woman—who was she? What had happened that night? The questions circled in my mind like vultures, waiting for the answers I didn't have. I clenched my fists, the sharp pain of my nails digging into my palms grounding me in the present.

My thoughts were interrupted by a sudden noise from the hallway. A floorboard creaked. My breath caught in my throat. I wasn't alone.

I slowly turned my head, scanning the darkness that seemed to stretch on forever. There was nothing there. Just shadows and the smell of damp wood, thick with mildew. But the noise had been real, I wasn't imagining it.

Who's there?

I forced my feet to move, creeping toward the doorway, my heart racing in anticipation. Every step I took echoed through the house, magnified in the stillness. The hairs on the back of my neck stood on end, my senses heightened to an almost painful degree. The darkness seemed to press in on me, thick and oppressive, as though the very house was closing in around me.

I reached the hallway. The old wooden floors groaned under my weight as I slowly advanced, my eyes darting from shadow to shadow, my breath coming in shallow gasps. There was no sound now, only the pounding of my heart.

I wasn't imagining things. Someone—or something—was here.

I reached the staircase and froze. The stairs led up into complete blackness, the upper floors swallowed by the void of the house's decay. I could hear faint whispers, like distant voices. A woman's laugh? A child crying? I couldn't tell. But I knew I wasn't alone.

Suddenly, a cold breeze swept down the staircase, ruffling my hair, and I felt it—a presence. I wasn't alone anymore. Something, someone, was waiting for me in the dark.

I didn't know what was worse—the oppressive silence, or the fact that something was moving in the shadows.

I glanced around, looking for a weapon. A chair, a broken piece of wood, anything to defend myself with. But there was nothing. Just the remnants of a life that had long since passed, now abandoned and forgotten. The walls seemed to close in as I stepped forward, the creaking floorboards growing louder with every movement.

Another sound.

A whisper.

It was closer now, unmistakable. A voice, low and raspy. "Eliza..."

My stomach flipped, and I took a step back. The voice had come from above. My pulse quickened as I realized I was being drawn upward, led by something, or someone. My body screamed for me to turn and run, but I couldn't. It was as if the house had ensnared me in its grip, and I was bound to follow its commands.

Eliza...

There it was again. The voice. But this time, it was different. It wasn't just a whisper. It was more urgent, more desperate, a plea that chilled me to the bone.

I forced myself to move, one slow step at a time, up the stairs. My breath was shallow, my heart thudding painfully in my chest. I had no idea what awaited me at the top, but I couldn't stop now. Not when the voice called to me, not when the house seemed to hold me captive.

As I reached the top of the stairs, the air grew colder, and the darkness felt like it was alive, wrapping around me like a shroud. There was no light here. No windows, no escape.

I took a deep breath and stepped forward. My hand brushed against the cold, crumbling wall, and I felt it—a sudden jolt of electricity, as if the house itself had come alive, reacting to my presence.

The whisper came again. Closer now. "Eliza, please..."

It was right behind me.

I spun around, my heart leaping into my throat.

But there was nothing.

Just the suffocating darkness, stretching on forever.

I turned back toward the end of the hall, but now there was a door—a door I was certain hadn't been there before. It was old, weathered, with a tarnished doorknob that gleamed in the faint light.

Without thinking, I reached for the handle. The door opened with a slow creak, as though it had been waiting for me to unlock it.

Inside was a room—empty, save for a single chair in the middle of the floor. The room was dark, but I could feel the weight of something watching me. I stepped inside.

And then the door slammed shut behind me.

I spun around, my hand grabbing for the handle, but the door wouldn't budge.

I was trapped.

And then, as the darkness closed in, I saw her again. The woman. The one whose voice had haunted me, whose words had burned themselves into my memory.

She was sitting in the chair, her eyes locked on mine.

"It's time, Eliza," she said softly, her voice a rasp in the silence. "It's time to remember what you've forgotten."

And the world went black.

29

The Secrets Beneath the Floorboards

The air was thick with the smell of mildew, as though the house itself had been forgotten by time, left to decay in the shadows of its own history. Eliza's breath came in shallow, quick gasps as she stood frozen in the room, the door behind her locked fast. Her pulse hammered in her ears, drowning out the silence that enveloped her, threatening to consume her. Every inch of her body screamed for escape, but the thick, suffocating air held her in place like an invisible force.

Her eyes darted to the figure sitting in the chair. The woman— who was she? What did she want? Eliza's mind raced, a thousand questions battling for dominance, but they all fell silent as the woman's gaze pierced through her, a hollow void behind her eyes.

Eliza could feel the weight of the room pressing down on her, as though the walls themselves were closing in. The woman's words still echoed in her ears, vibrating in the still air like an insistent whisper.

"It's time to remember what you've forgotten."

The words sent a chill racing down Eliza's spine. What was it that she had forgotten? Was it something she wanted to remember? Or something she'd desperately hoped to bury?

"You can't run from the past," the woman said again, her voice like gravel scraping against stone. There was a quiet finality to her tone, as though she had known Eliza's every move long before Eliza had even made them.

Eliza took a tentative step forward, her legs unsteady beneath her. She didn't know if it was fear or something deeper that made her hesitate, but she couldn't tear her eyes away from the woman's hollow stare.

"What do you want from me?" Eliza asked, her voice shaky but defiant. She didn't know where the words came from, but she had to speak. She had to break the suffocating silence that was threatening to engulf her.

The woman didn't answer immediately. Instead, she tilted her head to one side, as if considering Eliza's question, before slowly raising her hand, pointing toward the floor. The action was deliberate, slow, and in the silence of the room, it was as though the very gesture carried a heavy, unspoken message.

Eliza followed the woman's gaze, her heart skipping a beat as her eyes locked onto the floor beneath her feet. The floorboards were old, warped with age, but there was something off about them—something that made Eliza's pulse quicken. There, in the center of the floor, was a slight indentation, a subtle but unmistakable gap between two boards.

Without thinking, Eliza knelt down, her fingers trembling as she pried at the edges of the boards. The sound of splintering wood filled the room, echoing in her ears like a death knell, but she didn't stop. She had to know what was beneath them. Whatever the woman was trying to show her, whatever the house was hiding, Eliza had to face it head-on.

Her fingers finally grasped the edge of a loose board and pried it free. The moment it shifted, a rush of cold air seemed to seep from the gap, as if the house itself were exhaling, releasing the weight of its secrets. Eliza's breath caught in her throat as she peered into the dark space beneath the floor.

Something gleamed in the faint light—something metallic. She reached in, her hand trembling as she grasped the object. It was small, cold to the touch, and as she pulled it free, she gasped.

A key. An old, tarnished key.

Her mind raced. What was this for? Why had it been hidden here, beneath the floorboards? She had to know.

She turned the key over in her hand, studying it closely. It felt wrong somehow, as if it had been waiting for her. The weight of it in her palm seemed to pulse with a dark energy, something ancient, something that had been buried for far too long.

A sharp, sudden noise broke through the tension. The door—

behind her, the one she had thought was locked—creaked open, slowly, the hinges protesting against the silence. Eliza's heart stopped. She hadn't touched it. No one had come in. And yet, the door was moving on its own.

A figure stood in the doorway.

Eliza's stomach dropped.

She recognized him. It was the man from her dreams—the one who had been chasing her, who had haunted her thoughts in the dead of night. His eyes were cold, calculating, and his smile was a crooked, dangerous thing that sent a wave of nausea washing over her.

"You shouldn't have done that," he said, his voice low and menacing, sending a shiver down her spine. "You shouldn't have opened that door."

Eliza's mind spun. How did he know? She hadn't even realized there was another door.

Her hand tightened around the key, her knuckles white. She needed to escape. This couldn't be happening. She wasn't ready for this. She wasn't ready for the truth, for whatever had been hidden in this house, for the secrets that had been buried for so long. But she had no choice. She had to face it.

The man stepped into the room, his presence filling the space with an oppressive weight. Eliza could barely breathe, her chest constricting as he moved closer, his eyes never leaving her.

"You don't know what you've unleashed," he whispered, his voice like a snake slithering in the dark. "But you will. You'll wish you never found that key."

She didn't know what he meant, but she could feel it—the weight of something ancient and powerful, something dark and twisted that was now awake, reaching out from the shadows.

"No," Eliza whispered, her voice trembling as she stepped backward, instinctively moving toward the only exit—the door she'd just unlocked. But before she could make it, the man lunged forward, his hand grabbing her wrist with an iron grip.

Her heart pounded in her chest as she struggled, but his hold was unyielding.

"You can't run anymore," he said, his grin widening. "The past has already found you."

And then, just as Eliza thought she might collapse under the weight of it all, the room went cold. A chill that cut through her bones and stole the very breath from her lungs.

The woman in the chair, the one who had been silent all this time, spoke again, her voice a haunting whisper that seemed to come from all directions at once.

"It's too late, Eliza. The truth is already here."

And the room seemed to close in on her, the walls pressing tighter, the shadows dancing like living things around her.

There was no escape. The secrets beneath the floorboards were about to be unleashed.

30

The Echoes of the Forgotten

Eliza's breath was ragged, her heart hammering against her ribs as she struggled against the grip of the man's hand on her wrist. The weight of his touch was like a vice, and the coldness of it seemed to seep into her very bones. She twisted, desperately trying to free herself, but his hold only tightened.

"Let me go!" she gasped, her voice raw with panic. The fear that had been gnawing at her insides since she had stepped into this cursed house now threatened to swallow her whole.

But the man didn't respond. His expression remained eerily calm, a twisted smile curling at the corners of his lips as if he were savoring the terror that gripped her. His eyes—cold and distant—burned into her with a knowing intensity, as if he already understood everything about her, everything she had yet to uncover.

The woman in the chair, the one who had watched silently, now let out a low, almost imperceptible laugh, her voice croaking in the stillness. "You think you can outrun the truth, Eliza? You think you can hide from what you've forgotten?"

Eliza's mind raced, trying to make sense of what was happening. Who were these people? What were they trying to tell her? What had been hidden in this house for so long? The key in her hand felt heavier than ever, its jagged edges biting into her palm as if it were urging her to act. But act how? What could she do against the man who held her captive, against the weight of this oppressive, suffocating house?

"You have no idea what you're dealing with," the man said, his voice low, almost affectionate, like a predator toying with its prey. He leaned closer, his breath cold against her ear, sending a shiver down her spine. "You've opened the door. Now there's no going back."

Eliza's mind flashed back to that moment—when the floorboards had cracked beneath her fingers, when she had uncovered the key. The key to what? What was it unlocking? What was it leading her to?

"The house remembers, Eliza. It always remembers."

Suddenly, the air in the room seemed to grow colder, denser, as if the very walls were closing in on her. The shadows around them stretched long, curling and twisting like dark tendrils seeking to entrap her. It was as though the house itself had come alive, responding to the woman's words, to the man's presence.

The woman in the chair tilted her head back, the soft rustle of her clothing the only sound in the otherwise silent room. Eliza tried to tug her arm free again, but the man's grip was unyielding. The cold that seeped from him seemed to travel deeper, wrapping itself around her heart, constricting, squeezing.

"Stop!" Eliza cried out, her voice trembling as she looked toward the woman in the chair. "Tell me what's going on! What's happening to me? What do you want?"

The woman's lips parted slightly, and for a moment, Eliza thought she might answer. But then the woman's eyes flickered toward the door behind Eliza, and a chill passed through the room. The silence seemed to stretch in an unbearable tension before the woman spoke, her voice cold and clipped.

"You'll see soon enough. The past doesn't let go. And neither will he."

Before Eliza could react, the man jerked her toward the center of the room, forcing her to her knees. The key in her hand burned, the weight of it pulling her gaze downward, to the floorboards, to the indentation that had led her here.

"You don't know what that key is for," the man said, his voice dripping with mock sympathy. "You don't even know what it means. But you will. You'll understand when the truth comes rushing back. And when it does, you won't be able to escape."

A dark laugh rumbled in his chest, echoing in the space around them.

Eliza's mind spun, her thoughts a whirlwind of confusion and fear. Was this all some kind of twisted game? Or was there something more sinister at play here? She glanced again at the woman, hoping for some kind of reassurance, but the woman's face was unreadable, her eyes blank, her lips drawn into a thin, almost imperceptible line.

"You can't outrun what's inside you," the woman whispered, her voice barely audible. "It's been with you all along, Eliza. You just had to remember."

Eliza's breath hitched. Remember. The word rang in her ears like a bell tolling in the distance. Remember what? What had she forgotten? What was she supposed to remember?

Her gaze dropped to the key in her hand once more. She had no choice. She had to open whatever door it unlocked, no matter how terrifying it seemed. It was the only way forward. The only way to understand what was happening, to understand why she had been drawn here.

She stood slowly, the man's grip loosening as she moved, though he didn't let go completely. She was ready now—ready to face whatever the key would unlock.

Eliza took a deep breath and turned toward the far side of the room, her eyes scanning the walls, the shadows. She couldn't explain why, but her body seemed to know exactly where the door was. It was as if something inside her was pulling her toward it, guiding her.

"No," the man hissed. "Don't open it. You'll regret it. You can't go back."

But Eliza wasn't listening. She was past the point of turning back now. She stepped forward, placing the key in the lock of the old, weathered door. The metal groaned as it slid into place, and with a single, final turn, the door creaked open.

A gust of cold air rushed through the room, swirling around her like a storm. The shadows that had been stretching across the walls now seemed to surge forward, coiling around her as if the darkness itself were alive. The room before her was a black void, an abyss that seemed to stretch on forever.

She took one final step forward, feeling the ground beneath her feet shift, and then—

Everything went black.

The last thing Eliza heard before the darkness overtook her was the woman's voice, soft but clear, echoing in the distance:

"You've opened the door. Now you must face what lies beyond it."

31

The Door That No One Should Open

Eliza woke with a start, her body jolting upright as her eyes snapped open. She gasped for air, her lungs desperate, her chest heaving as though she had been underwater. The room around her was different—darker, quieter. The air was thick with the smell of old wood and dust, and for a moment, she thought she was still trapped in the nightmare that had clung to her like a shadow.

But no. This wasn't the same place.

Her hand instinctively reached for the key that had been in her grasp when she opened the door, but it was gone. In its place was a soft, almost imperceptible hum, like the distant beat of a drum. Her heart raced as she took in her surroundings, her mind still reeling from the strange, oppressive void she had stepped into just moments before.

She wasn't alone.

She could feel it.

The room was dimly lit, the faint glow of an overhead bulb casting long, eerie shadows across the walls. The floor beneath her feet was cold, slick, like stone or concrete, and there was a faint rattle in the distance, like the sound of something heavy shifting in the dark. The air was heavy with the scent of damp earth, and the quiet that enveloped the space was almost suffocating.

Eliza's eyes darted around the room, trying to make sense of it, but everything felt wrong. The walls were bare except for a single, large mirror that hung opposite her. She took a step toward it, her feet silent on the cold floor. As she neared, the air around her seemed to grow thicker, more oppressive, and she could feel a growing sense of unease gnawing at her insides.

There was something about that mirror. It wasn't just its size or its cracked edges, nor the way it reflected the room back at her in distorted shapes—it was the eyes. Her own eyes. They didn't belong to her.

Eliza's breath caught in her throat as she stepped closer to the glass. The woman in the reflection was older, with dark, hollow eyes that seemed to know something she didn't. The woman's lips moved, but no sound reached Eliza's ears. Instead, it was as if the air itself had absorbed the words, carrying them straight into her soul.

"You should never have come."

The whisper echoed in her mind, but the reflection remained frozen, still staring back at her, unblinking. The woman in the mirror smiled then, but it wasn't a friendly smile—it was one filled with sorrow, with knowing. And then, in a flash, the woman's face contorted into something grotesque, her features twisted into an expression of anguish.

Eliza stumbled backward, her heart racing. Her legs felt weak beneath her, as though the weight of the moment had drained the very strength from her body. She looked around frantically, but the mirror's reflection remained unchanged. The figure was still there, still watching, still whispering those words she couldn't quite understand.

"You should never have come."

But what did it mean? What was she supposed to understand? Her mind spun, trying to connect the dots—everything that had led her here, everything she had uncovered about her past, about the house, about the key—but it all felt fragmented, like pieces of a puzzle scattered across the floor. There was something more—something deeper—but Eliza couldn't grasp it, couldn't pull it all together.

She turned away from the mirror, her gaze now falling on the door she had entered through. It was still there, its wood dark and weathered, the keyhole in the center like an eye, watching her. But when she stepped toward it, she realized it didn't open the same way. It wouldn't budge, no matter how hard she pushed, no matter how hard she tried.

Trapped.

The word echoed in her mind like a warning, a whisper that had been buried deep within her for too long. She turned back to the mirror, her hands shaking as she gripped the edge of the cold, stone-like surface. Why had she opened it?

And then she heard it again.

The faint rattle, louder this time. Closer.

Eliza froze, her breath catching in her throat. She spun toward the source of the sound, but the room was still empty. Nothing moved. Nothing changed. But the noise grew louder, like the sound of chains scraping against the stone, the echoes of something ancient and long-forgotten.

She took a cautious step forward, her eyes scanning the dark corners of the room. And then she saw it—a shape, emerging from the shadows. It was like a figure, but it wasn't quite human. It was too tall, too thin, its limbs elongated and contorted. Its face—if it could be called that—was hidden in the shadows, but Eliza could see its eyes.

Dark. Empty.

Hollow.

The figure stepped closer, its movements unnaturally slow, as if savoring every moment, every inch of Eliza's growing terror.

"You should never have come."

The voice was louder now, clearer. The words seemed to come from everywhere—inside her head, around the room, echoing in the very air. It wasn't just a warning. It was a sentence.

Eliza staggered backward, her legs threatening to give way beneath her. Her eyes darted to the door again, but it was no use. She was trapped. She had no way out.

The figure reached out for her, its hand—clawed, skeletal—extended toward her with a deliberate slowness. She could feel the air change around her, thickening, pressing in on her, and for the first time, Eliza felt the weight of the house—of the curse it held—fully, deeply. This was no longer just about her past, no longer just about the key.

This was something far worse.

She turned to the mirror again, desperate to find something, anything, that might help. But all she saw was the reflection of herself—the woman with hollow eyes, now smiling cruelly at her.

"You can never escape."

The words echoed, and Eliza knew, with a sickening certainty, that they were true. There was no escape from this place, from the curse that had been laid upon her.

The figure stepped forward, its hand reaching closer, and Eliza could only watch, helpless, as the shadows swallowed her whole.

32

The Weight of Forgotten Secrets

Eliza's heart thudded in her chest as the cold, skeletal hand of the figure in the corner of the room reached for her. Her breath came in shallow gasps, panic threatening to drown her as the air around her thickened with something dark, something ancient. Her mind screamed for her to run, but her legs felt like they were rooted to the floor, as if some invisible force was holding her in place.

The figure's eyes, dark and hollow, gleamed with an unnerving sense of purpose. It wasn't human—she could feel that now, in every fiber of her being. It was something else, something born from the depths of forgotten shadows, a presence too powerful to be ignored.

The hand moved closer, and Eliza's pulse quickened. She had to move, had to escape—but the room felt smaller now, like the walls were closing in around her. Every step she tried to take toward the door felt futile, as though the very space itself was working against her. She could feel the weight of the room pressing on her, as if the walls, the mirror, the very air were conspiring to keep her trapped.

The figure's mouth moved, but the sound that came from it was not words—it was a low, rumbling growl that echoed deep within her chest. It was a sound that reverberated through her very bones, a vibration of terror she could feel more than hear.

You should never have opened the door.

The words whispered in her mind again, but this time, they weren't from the figure. They came from somewhere else— somewhere deeper, a voice that felt like it had been buried beneath layers of time. The voice was familiar. So familiar.

No...

Eliza shook her head, refusing to acknowledge the truth her heart was beginning to understand. The door. The mirror. The key. They were all part of it. Part of this terrible, twisted puzzle that had somehow led her back here.

The figure in the corner shifted, its movements slow, deliberate. The air grew colder, the shadows around it deepening, and Eliza could feel something ancient stirring in the darkness— something that had been waiting for her, something that had always been waiting for her.

She took a hesitant step back, but the figure's eyes followed her every movement, tracking her like a predator sensing its prey. The darkness in the room seemed to grow, swallowing every inch of light, until the entire space was nothing but a black void, save for the pale light cast by the mirror. The figure's hand moved again, its bony fingers stretching out toward her, and for a moment, Eliza thought she could hear the sound of chains rattling softly in the distance.

Run.

The voice was clearer now—urgent, desperate. But it wasn't just a voice. It was a memory.

Eliza's mind flashed back to a time long ago—a time when she had been younger, when her world had been simpler. She was standing in a field, the sun warm on her skin, the grass swaying gently in the breeze. She had been with someone, someone important. Someone who had warned her about the darkness, about the door.

Her breath caught in her throat as the memory crystallized in her mind. It was her mother's voice. The same voice that had once told her to never touch the door, to never open it, to never go near it.

The door.

Eliza's eyes flew to the door across the room, the one she had come through, the one that was now completely sealed shut. Her fingers tingled with the faintest touch of power, as though the key that had once been in her hand was still with her, hidden somewhere beneath the layers of fear and confusion.

You never should have opened it.

The voice was louder now, a chorus of whispers that seemed to come from everywhere, from every corner of the room, from every crack in the walls. The figure's hand was closer now, and Eliza could feel the chill of it in the air, like a frost creeping across the room. She turned to the mirror, her reflection no longer her own.

It was the woman—the woman she had seen before, the one with the hollow eyes, the one who had whispered those words to her earlier. But this time, there was no smile, no cruel twist to her face. This time, the woman in the mirror was staring at her with an intensity that made Eliza's skin crawl.

Leave, Eliza. Leave before it's too late.

The voice was her mother's again, but this time it was filled with an urgency that Eliza had never heard before.

You mustn't stay.

Eliza's pulse quickened, her mind racing as the weight of the moment pressed down on her. She was caught—caught between the past and the present, caught between the truth she had always known and the terrifying reality she was now facing. She had been warned. She had been warned, but she hadn't listened.

The figure in the corner of the room moved again, its skeletal frame shifting, its eyes gleaming with an unsettling hunger.

Eliza's throat went dry. There was nowhere to run. Nowhere to hide. The walls were closing in, and she could feel the darkness pressing closer, drawing her in.

And then, as if the room itself had answered her desperation, the floor beneath her feet began to tremble. It was subtle at first, a slight vibration that made the air hum, but it grew stronger with every passing second. The rattling noise grew louder, the sound of chains dragging across the floor growing nearer and nearer.

Eliza's eyes darted to the door again, and she could feel the key—her key—hidden deep within her. She knew she had to use it. She had to escape.

But then, the mirror shattered.

The glass splintered into thousands of shards, sending a shower of jagged fragments across the floor. Eliza gasped, her body instinctively jerking back. For a moment, she was paralyzed, staring at the remnants of the mirror, her reflection now broken, scattered across the room like a thousand shards of her own broken soul.

In the midst of the glass, something moved.

The figure.

It was emerging from the shattered mirror, its dark, hollow eyes glowing with an otherworldly light as it reached toward her, its bony fingers now inches from her face.

It's too late.

And in that instant, Eliza understood. The door, the key, the mirror, the figure—this was all a cycle. A trap that had been set long ago, and she was the one who had set it in motion.

She was the one who had opened the door.

33

The Depths of Silence

Eliza stood in the shattered remnants of the mirror, her breath coming in ragged gasps. The figure—its grotesque form now half-emerged from the pieces of glass—loomed before her, an embodiment of all the fear she had buried for years. Every shard of the mirror reflected its dark, hollow eyes, and with each reflection, Eliza felt herself unraveling further, the threads of her own sanity beginning to fray.

She backed away slowly, her feet scraping against the cold floor, the echoes of the broken glass underfoot like distant, mocking whispers. The air around her had thickened again, heavy with something thick and oppressive. It was the same feeling she had felt when she first arrived, that sense that the very room was watching her, waiting for her to make the wrong move. And now, every instinct within her screamed to run, to flee, but there was nowhere to go. The door was sealed, the room was a cage, and the figure in front of her moved with a predatory calm.

"Leave," the voice croaked from the figure's mouth, a voice that sounded like it was born from the very earth itself, ancient and gravelly. It was not a plea. It was a command. "You do not belong here."

Eliza shook her head, trying to clear the fog in her mind. This wasn't just any figure. It wasn't a random manifestation of fear. This... thing, this being, was tied to her, tied to her very existence. She had known it the moment she had seen its reflection in the mirror. The key, the door, the locked memories—everything had led her here. But why? Why had she been chosen? What was the true cost of uncovering the secrets she had long buried?

She swallowed, her voice trembling as she spoke, though she didn't know what she was asking. "What are you? What do you want from me?"

The figure's lips curled into a grin, too wide, too unnerving. "What do I want?" it repeated, its voice a soft, chilling laugh. "I want nothing. But you... You want everything, don't you?"

Eliza froze, the words piercing her heart like a cold dagger. The truth—sudden, undeniable—rushed through her mind. This wasn't just about breaking some ancient curse, or unraveling some forgotten family secret. No, it was much more personal than that. The figure didn't just reflect her fear; it reflected her deepest desires, her darkest, hidden yearnings.

She had wanted the truth. She had always wanted to know, to understand. But some truths came with a price, a cost far greater than she had ever imagined.

The figure stepped closer, its movements slow, deliberate, as if savoring the terror it saw in her eyes. The shadows seemed to deepen around it, swirling in a dark, malevolent dance. Eliza could feel the weight of its gaze on her, as though it were peeling back layers of her soul, exposing everything she had tried to hide. Everything she had tried to forget.

The mirror shards scattered at her feet seemed to hum, vibrating with some unknown energy. The room—the house—felt alive, as if it were shifting, growing, twisting with the very breath of the entity that now stood before her. The walls seemed to pulse with a low, rhythmic beat, and the faint sound of something dragging against the floor echoed in the distance.

The figure raised a hand, its long, skeletal fingers reaching out toward her, and Eliza instinctively stepped back, her heart racing. "What do you want from me?" she demanded again, the words coming out in a rasp.

The figure's grin widened, but there was no humor in it—only something far darker. "You want the truth, don't you? The truth of who you really are. The truth about what lies beneath all the lies you've told yourself. But the truth comes at a cost."

The room seemed to tilt, the floor beneath her feet no longer stable, as if gravity itself was bending. The door—still sealed, still impossible to open—mocked her from the far end of the room. She had been trapped here, but it wasn't just the physical space that held her captive. It was the truth—the truth that the figure was offering her, whether she wanted it or not.

Eliza closed her eyes, willing herself to hold on to some sliver of clarity. She didn't need this. She didn't need the past to rise up and swallow her whole. The truth, she realized, wasn't some grand revelation. It wasn't the key to some ancient mystery. The truth was something far simpler—and far more painful.

Her mind flashed to the memories she had tried so desperately to suppress, the memories that had been hidden behind locked doors for years. The betrayal. The lies. The secrets that her family had buried so deep that even she had begun to believe them. She had wanted to escape them, to outrun the suffocating darkness of them—but here it was, staring her in the face, demanding that she confront it.

The figure's voice pierced the silence again, and this time, it was colder, sharper. "You cannot hide. You cannot run. You will face the truth. You will face yourself."

Her heart pounded in her chest as the walls seemed to close in further. Eliza reached out a trembling hand, her fingers brushing against the broken mirror shards at her feet. She felt the cold, jagged edges of them, their sharpness like the thorns of a rose—dangerous, beautiful, and ultimately, deadly.

Suddenly, the floor beneath her feet gave way. She gasped as she felt herself falling, tumbling into the darkness. The air around her seemed to warp, distorting everything in its path. The light from the shattered mirror flickered, casting long, twisted shadows against the walls, and Eliza could hear the echo of the figure's voice, now distant, but still cutting through the air.

You cannot escape.

She tried to scream, but her voice was swallowed by the growing silence. The truth—the one truth she had been trying to outrun—was catching up with her. She had opened the door. She had unlocked the past. And now, the past was claiming her.

As she plummeted into the abyss, the only thing she could hear was the sound of her own heartbeat, thumping louder and louder until it filled her ears. And then, just before everything went black, the figure's final words echoed in her mind:

There is no way back.

The darkness consumed her.

34

The Echoes of Forgotten Dreams

Eliza's body crashed against the ground with a sickening thud, her breath forced out of her chest as the air knocked from her lungs. She lay there for a long moment, the world around her nothing but a dark blur of swirling shadows. The silence was oppressive, suffocating, as though the very air had thickened, become too dense to breathe.

Her head throbbed, the dizziness from her fall threatening to pull her under. She forced her eyes open, though the sight that greeted her did nothing to ease the tension curling like ice in her stomach. The floor beneath her wasn't solid—it seemed to shift, undulating, almost like she was lying on the surface of water. Dark, liquid shadows rippled around her, as though the darkness itself were alive.

Her heart pounded in her chest, her pulse erratic as she pushed herself up. Her hands scraped against something smooth but slick, the sensation almost unreal. The floor, no—was it the ground? Was she even still in the same place? She couldn't remember, the memories of the mirror room already fading into the haze of her mind.

"Eliza..." a whisper broke the silence, the voice like a distant echo, calling her name from somewhere far beyond her reach.

Her breath caught in her throat. It was familiar—so familiar. She had heard it before, but where? Who was it?

"Eliza..." The voice came again, stronger this time, but still soft, like a whisper in the wind. "Don't you remember?"

A shiver ran down her spine. The world around her seemed to tilt once more, the shadows bending and swirling like dark tendrils reaching out to claim her. She stood, unsteady, feeling as though she were caught in the grip of something far beyond her comprehension.

Her feet were bare, and she could feel the strange, wet surface beneath her, cold and unyielding. She had to move. She had to find her bearings before the darkness closed in.

"Eliza..."

The voice was louder now, insistent. It tugged at her, beckoning her toward something. She didn't know what it was, but she knew she had no choice but to follow it. Slowly, unsteadily, she took a step forward, her legs trembling beneath her. The shadows seemed to part, as though granting her passage, but she couldn't shake the feeling that something was watching her—something just beyond the edge of her perception.

The shadows pulled back, revealing what lay ahead.

A door. A simple, wooden door. It stood alone in the center of the void, untouched by the shifting darkness, as if it had always been there, waiting for her. Her breath hitched in her throat. She knew this door. She had seen it before. But where?

Eliza moved toward it, her feet sinking into the strange ground with each step. She felt her heart pounding in her chest, louder with each passing moment. The air around her seemed to grow heavier, the darkness pressing in from all sides. She reached out a hand, the coldness of the door sending a jolt through her. Her fingers brushed the surface, and the instant her skin made contact, the door seemed to tremble, as though alive.

The voice came again, this time desperate, pleading. "Eliza, don't open it. Don't open the door."

Eliza froze, her breath catching in her throat. She knew that voice too. It was hers—her own voice, but twisted, distorted. She had heard it many times, always in moments of weakness, in the darkest corners of her mind. It was the voice that warned her, the voice that always told her to stop, to turn back before it was too late.

But she couldn't. Something deep within her—something insistent—told her that she had to open the door. She had to know what lay beyond it, had to confront whatever truth it held.

With trembling hands, she pushed the door open, its hinges

creaking in protest, as though reluctant to let her through.

The scene that awaited her on the other side was not what she expected. It was... familiar. Too familiar.

She stepped into the room, her breath hitching in her throat. The walls were lined with bookshelves, their shelves heavy with volumes she recognized but couldn't place. The room smelled of dust and old paper, the air thick with the scent of something forgotten. It was as though she had stepped into a memory, into a time she could not quite recall.

"Eliza..." The voice called to her again, softer now, almost gentle. But it carried with it a weight, a sorrow that pressed against her chest, squeezing the air from her lungs. "Come closer..."

Her legs moved of their own accord, carrying her deeper into the room, toward a desk at the far end. Upon it sat an old, leather-bound journal. She knew it. She had seen it before—many times, in dreams and fleeting glimpses of memory. It was hers, wasn't it? Her journal, the one she had kept when she was younger, the one she had hidden away and forgotten.

But why? Why had she forgotten?

Her fingers trembled as she reached for it, the journal warm against her touch. The moment her fingers brushed its surface, a jolt of recognition hit her like a bolt of lightning. The memories flooded back in an overwhelming rush, crashing through her mind, threatening to drown her.

Her younger self—sitting at the desk, writing feverishly, trying to make sense of the chaos that had consumed her life. The whispers of a past she had been too afraid to confront, the shadows of forgotten dreams that had once haunted her every night. She had tried to escape them, to bury them, but they were here now, standing before her, demanding to be remembered.

As she opened the journal, a single piece of paper fluttered from its pages. She caught it just before it hit the ground, her breath catching in her throat as she read the words written in familiar, shaky handwriting:

"You are not who you think you are. You are the key to all of this."

The room seemed to close in around her, the shadows thickening as the air grew colder. The voice, now a chorus of whispers, filled her ears, its words unspoken yet understood.

You must face it. You must remember.

And then, with a suddenness that made her heart lurch in her chest, the journal vanished, dissolving into the shadows. The room was empty again—silent, still. The door she had entered through was gone, leaving her trapped in the suffocating darkness.

But somewhere in the distance, she could hear it—the sound of footsteps, approaching slowly, steadily. And with each step, the whisper grew louder.

You cannot escape.

Her heart raced, panic rising in her chest as the footsteps grew closer. There was nowhere to run, nowhere to hide. The truth was coming for her, and this time, there would be no turning back.

35

The Path Beneath the Moon

Eliza's breath was ragged as she stood at the edge of the cliff, staring down into the abyss below. The wind whipped through her hair, tugging at her, but she remained still, her eyes locked on the blackness. The darkness seemed endless, like an ocean of night, pulling her in with an invisible force. The moon, full and haunting, hung low in the sky, casting an eerie glow over the scene. It was the only light in the vast emptiness, and yet it seemed to deepen the shadows rather than dispel them.

She could feel something closing in around her, as though the very earth was shifting beneath her feet. The ground trembled slightly, a subtle vibration that sent a chill crawling up her spine. She had been here before—she knew it. The cliffs, the moon, the oppressive weight of silence. This was the place where it all began, the place where her memories had fractured into a million shards, each one sharp and painful, each one leading her back to this moment.

The wind howled again, louder this time, carrying with it a

strange whisper. It was familiar, but distorted, like a memory echoing through time, its meaning slipping just beyond her grasp. She closed her eyes, trying to catch the fragments, but they dissolved the moment she tried to hold on.

"Eliza..."

The voice, soft yet commanding, slid into her consciousness, and she froze. It was him. She could feel it in her bones. The voice that had haunted her dreams, the voice that had followed her through the corridors of her mind, now finally calling her into the unknown.

"Eliza..." The voice was closer now, insistent, its sound like the rustling of leaves in the wind, a haunting melody woven through with an undercurrent of urgency.

She opened her eyes, scanning the dark horizon. There was no sign of anyone, no movement in the shadows, but she knew— she could feel him there. He was close. So close. Her heart began to race, her pulse quickening in her throat.

The footsteps came next—soft, deliberate, echoing across the stillness of the night. They were unmistakable. His. She had heard them before, in another time, in another place. They were the footsteps of a man who had walked alongside her in her dreams, a man whose presence had always lingered just out of reach.

"Eliza..." The voice was now right behind her, and despite every instinct in her body telling her to turn, to flee, she remained frozen, as if her very soul had been anchored to the spot.

She felt his presence more than she saw it, a dark weight pressing against her back, a shadow falling over her that threatened to swallow her whole. The wind died down, and with it, the world seemed to hold its breath.

"You've come to the edge," the voice whispered. "But do you know what lies beyond?"

Eliza closed her eyes again, trying to steady her breath. The darkness in front of her felt alive, as though it were watching her, waiting for her to make a choice. The abyss beckoned, its depths calling her name like a siren song, offering her a release from the overwhelming confusion that had consumed her for so long.

But what was she supposed to do? Was she supposed to leap into it, to surrender to the shadows? Or was this a test—another puzzle to solve, another fragment of her fractured memories that needed to be pieced together?

The whispering voice grew louder, more insistent. "It's always been this way, hasn't it, Eliza? The unknown calling to you, the secrets hidden in the darkness. You've run from them, hidden from the truth. But now... now you must face it."

Her eyes snapped open. There, just in front of her, was the figure she had been waiting for—the man whose presence had lingered like smoke in her thoughts. He stood at the edge of the cliff, his back to her, looking out over the abyss. He was tall, his silhouette dark against the moonlight, his features obscured by the shadows.

"Eliza..." He turned slowly, his voice cutting through the air like a blade. "I've been waiting for you."

Her heart skipped a beat. The moment his eyes met hers, everything shifted. The world around her seemed to blur, the edges of reality warping as though the very fabric of space and time were bending. She tried to speak, but no words came. She was frozen, unable to move, unable to breathe.

"You've come to find me," he said, his voice softer now, tinged with something Eliza couldn't quite place. Was it sadness? Longing? "But do you know what you're really looking for?"

She opened her mouth to reply, but again, nothing came. The silence stretched between them, thick and oppressive, as though the very air had become heavy with the weight of unspoken truths.

He took a step toward her, his movements slow and deliberate. As he came closer, Eliza could feel the tension between them, a crackling energy that seemed to pulse in the air. Her chest tightened, and for the first time in what felt like forever, a sense of clarity washed over her.

"I've been lost for so long," she whispered, her voice hoarse. "I don't know what's real anymore. I don't know who I am."

His gaze softened, and he reached out, his hand hovering just inches from hers. His fingers trembled as if he, too, was unsure of what to do, unsure of the path they were both standing on.

"You are not lost, Eliza," he said gently. "You've always known who you are. You just... forgot."

The words hit her like a punch to the gut. She staggered back, her mind racing, her heart hammering in her chest. Forgot. The word echoed in her mind, reverberating with a sense of finality, like the closing of a door she had never known was open.

"Forgot?" she repeated, her voice rising with disbelief. "I've never forgotten. I've been searching for something—someone—this whole time. I—I need to know who you are!"

He smiled, but it wasn't a smile of reassurance. It was something darker, something laden with secrets. "I'm the one you've been running from, Eliza. And now, you're here. You're finally ready."

Her eyes narrowed, suspicion rising within her. "Ready for what?"

The man stepped forward, closing the distance between them in a single stride. "Ready to face the truth."

And with that, everything began to unravel. The moon above flickered, casting strange, twisted shadows across the cliff. The ground beneath her feet trembled again, and the wind began to howl as though the earth itself were waking from a long, restless sleep.

"Eliza," the man whispered, his voice barely audible over the wind. "The path beneath the moon is the one you must walk. The one you were always meant to walk."

She felt the pull then—the undeniable force drawing her toward him, toward the abyss. The secrets, the answers, everything she had been searching for, were just beyond her reach. But in order to take that final step, she would have to surrender.

And as she did, she realized with a sickening clarity—there was no turning back.

36

The Veil of Forgotten Truths

The rain had started softly, a gentle patter that soon became a downpour, hammering against the stones beneath Eliza's feet. She could hear it in the air before she felt the first drop—a heavy stillness, like the world was bracing itself for something inevitable. The cliffside had been swept in shadow, the full moon no longer visible as thick clouds rolled over it, thick and unyielding. Everything was submerged in darkness. The kind of darkness that pressed against her, filling her lungs with the scent of wet earth, of things hidden beneath the surface.

"Eliza…" The voice was barely a whisper, but she heard it as clearly as if it were shouted into her ear. She turned sharply, her pulse quickening. It wasn't his voice—at least not in the way she had grown accustomed to. It was different, fractured. Distant, yet right beside her.

She reached for the familiar comfort of her thoughts, trying to steady herself. But her mind was as tangled as the branches swaying in the wind.

There was something here—a presence. She could feel it in the pit of her stomach, that cold, tightening sensation that came just before a storm. Her heart thudded in her chest as she scanned the shadows, but saw nothing.

Nothing.

The words were there, though, in the air—woven into the silence like a tapestry she couldn't quite make sense of.

"Eliza..."

It came again, clearer this time. Not his voice—someone else's. But still, it felt like a call. A summons.

"Who's there?" Her voice trembled as she stepped forward, her hands shaking as the cold rain drenched her skin. She glanced back toward the figure standing at the edge of the cliff. His presence, once steady and comforting, had faded into the night, a shadow among shadows.

"Eliza, you don't remember, do you?" The voice was not just in her ears now; it was inside her head, echoing through her skull like the turning of a forgotten key in a locked door.

She froze. A rush of memories hit her like a wave—brief flashes of light, moments so vivid they seemed to be unfolding before her very eyes.

The house on the hill.
   The photograph with the torn corner.

The letter that never made it to the mailbox.

Her breath hitched. What was happening? Why was this feeling so familiar?

"Eliza..." The voice continued, softer now, coaxing. "Come closer. All the answers you need are here."

She wanted to turn away. She wanted to run. But something inside her wouldn't let her. Curiosity. Need. She didn't know what she was searching for, but she knew it was just within reach. It had always been just out of her grasp, and now—now it was calling her.

Slowly, she stepped toward the edge of the cliff.

The rain fell harder, pounding the earth with a deafening roar. The winds whipped at her face, lashing at her skin, but she didn't flinch. It was like the storm itself had become a part of her—part of the restless energy gnawing at the edges of her memory.

She reached the precipice, her feet trembling on the slick rock. Below her, the abyss stretched endlessly into the void, like the gaping mouth of some ancient creature ready to swallow her whole. She didn't look down. She couldn't.

"Eliza, don't be afraid."

The voice was clear now, and as it echoed in her ears, it twisted. She knew this voice. Knew it better than any other.

Her eyes widened as recognition washed over her.

It was him. The man who had stood before her on this very cliff. The one who had promised answers.

He wasn't here now, not in the flesh. But his voice—it was everywhere. It surrounded her like a fog, its tendrils curling around her mind, tightening the grip around her heart.

"You've always known, haven't you?" The voice urged. "You've always known the truth, Eliza. But you've hidden it away. Buried it. You were afraid to face it. Afraid of what it would mean."

She gasped, her hands trembling as she clutched the edge of the stone, leaning forward as if the words alone could pull her into the darkness.

"Stop," she whispered, her voice choked with the weight of it. "Stop. I don't want to know."

But it was too late. The floodgates had opened. The truth was rushing toward her, a torrent of memories crashing against her, pushing her to the edge.

"No, Eliza," the voice continued, its calm tone now laced with something darker. "You've always wanted to know. You've been searching for it in every shadow, every whisper. The past is never truly buried. It waits for you to remember."

Her breath caught in her throat. The past. Her past. The

fractured pieces that had never quite fit, that had always been out of place—suddenly, they began to slot together, one by one. She saw the images more clearly now. The house. The photograph. The letter.

The man.

Her heart skipped. The memories—so sharp, so real—rushed toward her. She could feel her pulse quicken as the pieces connected. He had been there. The man she had once known, the man whose face had slipped away from her like smoke.

And now she understood.

The memories had never left her. She had buried them, locked them in a place too deep to remember. But now, the weight of them was crashing through. The truth, buried beneath years of denial, was forcing its way back into her life.

Why had she forgotten?

"Eliza..." The voice was now a soft, mocking caress, brushing against her like a lover's breath. "You can't outrun the truth. Not anymore."

With a sharp intake of breath, Eliza turned, her hands pressed against her ears as if she could block it out. But the voice was inside her. Inside her bones.

She staggered backward, her body trembling as the memories flooded her all at once. Her heart slammed against her chest, and her vision swam.

A house. Her childhood home. A secret. A betrayal.

A man—his face emerging through the haze of her past. His eyes, cold and calculating. And a memory, buried so deep, so well hidden—until now. A betrayal so intimate, so heart-wrenching, she could hardly breathe.

Her vision blurred, and for a moment, she thought she might collapse.

"Eliza..." the voice murmured, almost a whisper, like a lover's last breath. "Remember me. Remember us."

The sky above her flashed with a blinding light, a jagged bolt of lightning splitting the darkness. And in that instant, everything froze.

Eliza gasped, her hands shaking violently as she stumbled backward, her heart pounding in her chest. The truth, now exposed, had come alive within her—flooding her soul with a terrifying understanding.

The storm raged on.

37

The Last Whisper of the Past

The heavy scent of damp earth hung in the air as Eliza stood before the old oak door, the one she had avoided for years. It loomed like a silent sentinel, its dark wood weathered by time and secrecy. The hinges were rusty, and the faintest creak echoed in the stillness as she placed a trembling hand on the cold brass knob.

She had always known it was here, tucked away at the farthest corner of her father's estate. Locked. Guarded. Waiting. And yet, for years, she had never dared approach it. Every whisper in her childhood—every faint echo of a memory—had warned her to stay away. But now, as the storm raged outside and the sky cracked with thunder, she had no choice but to face it.

"Why now?" she whispered under her breath, barely audible against the pounding rain. Her chest tightened, as though her very soul knew what lay on the other side. But she didn't wait for an answer. She had already come too far.

The door creaked open, the sound echoing through the vast, empty hallway of her childhood home. The air inside was thick with dust, and the faintest chill seemed to seep from the walls. She stepped over the threshold, her heart racing in her chest. She could feel the weight of the house pressing down on her, like a memory that refused to fade. The grand staircase loomed before her, casting long shadows down the length of the corridor.

Each step she took seemed to reverberate through the silence, amplifying the sense of something lurking in the darkness. She swallowed hard, the taste of fear bitter in her mouth. There was a heaviness in the air, like the house itself was holding its breath. The floor beneath her feet creaked under the strain, the sound unnervingly loud in the otherwise oppressive silence.

Eliza's breath quickened as she moved deeper into the heart of the house. The walls were lined with portraits, the faces of long-dead ancestors staring down at her with eyes that seemed to follow her every move. Their cold, painted gazes were a reminder of everything she had tried to forget—of every secret that had been buried beneath layers of lies.

She rounded the corner into the drawing room, her pulse quickening with each step. The old furniture was covered in white sheets, their outlines faintly visible in the dim light. The faint smell of mildew lingered in the air, mingling with the scent of old wood and stale air. It was as though time had stood still here, leaving everything to rot in its wake.

But there was something else. Something darker. She could

feel it pressing against her chest, thick and suffocating.

As she reached the center of the room, her gaze fell upon the ornate fireplace, the hearth now cold and empty. And then she saw it—a small, leather-bound book, lying on the mantle. It was as though it had been waiting for her. She hesitated for a moment, her breath caught in her throat. This was it. This was the thing she had been avoiding. The thing that had always been there, just out of reach.

Her hand trembled as she reached out to touch the book. The moment her fingers made contact with the cool leather, a surge of energy shot through her, like an electric jolt. She recoiled, but it was too late. The past had already begun to uncoil itself inside her, filling her mind with images and voices from long ago.

"You can't run from the truth forever, Eliza."

Her father's voice echoed in her mind, cold and unyielding. The memory of his eyes—sharp, calculating—flashed before her. The man who had raised her, and yet, had never truly been hers. The man who had hidden so much from her, and yet expected her to be blind to it all.

She opened the book, her hands shaking violently. The pages were yellowed with age, the ink faded but legible. The words seemed to blur before her eyes, but she forced herself to focus. Each letter, each line, was a ghost rising from the depths of her past. And as she read, the memories—dark, twisted—began to crawl from the shadows.

"Eliza… your mother's death was no accident. It was a plan. A plan that I was a part of."

She gasped, the words searing through her mind like a brand. Her breath caught in her throat. Her mother. Her death. The lies that had surrounded it. Everything she had been told—the story she had believed—was a lie.

"Why?" she whispered, the word slipping from her lips without thought. "Why would you do this?"

The book remained open in her hands, as though the answer was right there, waiting for her. But the words didn't come. Instead, a noise—soft, almost imperceptible—flickered in the silence. It was a breath. A whisper. A voice she had not heard in years.

"Eliza…"

Her heart stopped.

It was his voice. The man she had left behind. The man she had come to think was gone forever. She spun around, her eyes scanning the room, but there was nothing. No one. Just the shadows stretching across the walls. The sound of the storm outside, the rain crashing against the windows.

"Eliza…"

The voice again, clearer now, and closer. She felt it. He was here.

The room spun around her. She was trapped between the past and the present, between the lies she had believed and the terrible truth that had now been revealed. The walls were closing in, the air thick with an electric charge that made her skin prickle.

Her breath was shallow, her chest tight. She wanted to scream, to run. But something—something held her there. The past was calling her, pulling her deeper into its tangled web of secrets. She could no longer escape. She could no longer deny it.

"Eliza, you need to listen." The voice was right behind her now, a whisper in the dark. "You've always known, but now it's time to remember."

The book in her hands trembled, its pages turning on their own, as though the book itself was alive. And as the words began to take shape, as the past bled into the present, Eliza understood. She understood everything.

But the truth came with a price. The price was far higher than she had ever imagined.

38

Beneath the Weight of Silence

The sound of the storm outside had faded into a distant rumble, swallowed up by the heavy quiet of the mansion. Eliza stood frozen in the drawing room, the old leather-bound book still open in her hands, its pages fluttering as though alive. The weight of the words she had just read pressed on her chest, thick and suffocating. It felt as though the walls themselves were closing in, trapping her within a past she had never truly known.

She was no longer alone. The air had shifted, thickened with a presence she couldn't see but could feel crawling up her spine like cold fingers. She wanted to turn, to look, but fear held her in place, anchoring her feet to the floor.

"Who's there?" Her voice was barely a whisper, swallowed by the oppressive silence. Her breath came in shallow bursts, her heart thundering in her chest as if it, too, had sensed the presence.

No answer. But the feeling grew stronger, a shadow weaving in and out of the corner of her vision, something familiar yet unknowable. Her eyes darted around the room, scanning for any sign of movement, but everything remained still—too still.

"Eliza..." The voice came again, a rasping whisper, so close it made the hairs on the back of her neck stand at attention.

This time, she couldn't ignore it. She spun around, her body trembling with the force of the sudden motion. The room was empty. There was no one there, no figure standing in the doorway or lingering in the shadows. But she could feel the gaze upon her—cold, watching.

Her pulse quickened, panic beginning to claw at her throat. She wanted to leave, to run out into the storm where at least she could feel the rain, the air, something that was real. But the door, the one she had come through only moments ago, now seemed like an impossible distance away.

"Eliza..."

This time, the voice was not a whisper. It was low, desperate, like a plea from deep within the walls themselves. It came from everywhere, swirling around her like a haunting wind.

Her eyes fell to the book still clutched in her hands, the pages turning of their own accord. As if compelled by an unseen force, she stepped forward, her feet moving despite her better judgment. The words on the page blurred before her, the ink smudging into illegible shapes, but one word remained clear:

Remember.

The word hit her like a punch to the gut. Her hands shook violently as she held the book tighter, her knuckles white. Remember what? She could barely breathe, as if the very act of looking at the book threatened to swallow her whole. It felt wrong—everything about it felt wrong—but the pull of the past was too strong, like a gravity that had caught her in its thrall.

Suddenly, the air shifted again. A cold wind swept through the room, rustling the white sheets that covered the old furniture. A gust of air slammed the windows shut with a deafening crash, and the book in her hands jerked as though yanked by an unseen hand. The pages stopped turning, and Eliza was left staring at the final paragraph that had come into focus just moments before.

You were never meant to know. But now, you must. It's time to face the truth.

Her breath hitched. The words were clear now, the truth she had avoided her entire life sitting before her in ink and paper. She could feel it deep in her bones—an undeniable truth she had long suspected but never allowed herself to believe.

The floorboards creaked behind her.

Her heart skipped a beat.

Someone was in the room.

"Eliza..." The voice came again, closer now. It was no longer a whisper. It was a low, guttural rasp that seemed to echo from deep within the house, rising from the very foundation of the mansion itself. It was familiar, too familiar.

She spun around, her body aching with the force of the movement. The shadow in the corner of the room seemed to shift, just a flicker of movement, but it was enough to make her freeze.

"Eliza..." It was him. Her father. But it couldn't be. He was dead. She had buried him herself. She had mourned him.

"Eliza..." The voice again, but now it was a command. "Come."

The word was no longer a suggestion. It was an order—impossible to ignore. She couldn't tell if the voice was real or if it was only her mind unraveling beneath the weight of what she had just learned. But her feet were moving, her legs carrying her toward the dark corner of the room, where the shadows gathered thickest.

And then, in a movement so sudden she could barely process it, the figure appeared. It was him—her father. But it wasn't him, not really. His face was gaunt, his eyes hollow, as though the very life had been drained from him. His body was translucent, like smoke that wavered in the dim light, but his presence was unmistakable.

"Eliza, you've come to understand," he said, his voice a rasping whisper, distant and cold. "Now, you must listen."

She opened her mouth to speak, to scream, to run, but no sound emerged. Her voice was lost somewhere within the overwhelming silence that enveloped her.

"You think you know the truth, don't you?" His voice deepened, an eerie calmness in his tone. "But the truth is more than you can bear. It's a burden. A legacy. And it will never let you go."

The room spun. The walls seemed to close in, pressing in on her until she could no longer breathe. The shadows stretched out toward her, hungry and cold.

She took a step back, then another, but her feet were heavy, as though the very ground beneath her was holding her in place. She was trapped.

And then, just as quickly as he had appeared, the figure began to fade, like smoke slipping through her fingers.

"Eliza..." the voice lingered one last time, as though a final warning, before the darkness swallowed it whole.

The room fell silent once more.

She was alone again. But not truly alone. Something had changed. The past had caught up to her, and it was no longer a secret buried in the past. It was alive, breathing, and waiting for her to make her next move.

"Eliza, it's time," the words echoed in her mind, a warning that could not be ignored.

But she was ready now. She had no choice but to face it. The truth. The legacy. And whatever came next.

39

The Echo of the Forgotten

The wind howled outside, rattling the windows as if trying to break into the house. Eliza stood motionless, her hands gripping the book tightly, her fingers trembling. Her heart pounded like a drumbeat in her chest, each thud reminding her of the terrifying truth she had uncovered. The shadows in the room seemed to stretch and writhe around her, as though the darkness itself was alive, watching her every move.

She had never felt so alone. The house, once a place of memories and fleeting comfort, now felt like a cage, its walls closing in on her. She could hear nothing but the relentless storm outside and the sound of her own breath, shallow and rapid.

It's time to face the truth, the voice had said. The words echoed in her mind, too loud to ignore. But what did that even mean? What was the truth? She had thought she knew the answers, had convinced herself that the past was buried, locked away in the corners of this decaying mansion. But now, the past was no longer something she could keep hidden. It had crawled out, wrapped its fingers around her throat, and forced her to confront it.

Eliza closed her eyes for a moment, her pulse still racing. She could still feel the cold touch of her father's presence lingering in the room, could still hear his voice, raspy and hollow, telling her that she was part of something far darker than she could ever understand. A legacy. The word lingered, burning through her thoughts like acid. What legacy? What had he meant?

Without thinking, she found herself walking toward the farthest corner of the room, the shadows growing thicker with every step she took. The house seemed to groan around her, as though it, too, was trying to remember something long forgotten. The air was thick with the scent of mildew, dust, and something else—something ancient, decayed, almost... malevolent.

There, in the corner of the room, hidden beneath layers of dust and cobwebs, was an old wooden chest. Eliza froze. Her eyes locked on it, her breath catching in her throat. She had never noticed it before, never seen it in any of her childhood memories of this place. But it was here now, standing at the edge of her consciousness, daring her to open it.

She swallowed hard, stepping closer, her feet dragging across the creaky floorboards. The chest was old, its wood worn and chipped, its hinges rusted. But the lock was still intact, an intricate iron clasp that seemed to gleam in the dim light. The sight of it made her stomach twist, but she couldn't pull away.

She had to know.

Reaching out, her fingers brushed against the cold metal of the lock. The moment her skin made contact, a flash of something—something dark and terrifying—rushed through her, like a flood of memories she couldn't control. Her vision blurred for a split second, and she stumbled back, gasping for air.

No. Not yet.

But the pull was irresistible. The voice, the shadows, the secrets—they were all calling to her. She needed to know. Whatever was hidden inside that chest was the key to understanding everything. Her past, her father, the mysterious legacy that seemed to haunt every step she had taken.

With trembling hands, she fumbled for the key. Her fingers brushed against the cold metal, and for a moment, it felt like the chest was laughing at her, mocking her desperation. But then, finally, her hand closed around the key that hung from the chain around her neck—the key her mother had worn for years, never telling her what it unlocked, only that it was something important, something that would reveal itself when the time was right.

Eliza inserted the key into the lock. There was a moment of resistance, as though the chest was fighting her, but then, with a soft click, the lock gave way. Her breath caught in her throat, her pulse pounding in her ears. Slowly, she lifted the lid, and the smell of old paper and something rotting wafted up, making her stomach churn.

Inside the chest, there were old documents, brittle and yellowed with age. Letters, faded photographs, and—at the very bottom—something wrapped in a dark cloth. The cloth was stained with age, but it didn't hide the shape of the object beneath it. It was something long, thin, and cold to the touch.

Eliza's fingers shook as she reached for the bundle. She unfolded the cloth, and what she found inside made her blood run cold.

A knife.

It was an old blade, intricately carved, with a handle wrapped in dark leather. The steel gleamed faintly in the dim light, its surface reflecting something... something Eliza couldn't quite understand. The weight of the blade in her hand felt wrong, like it was a part of her—a part of the family she had never truly known.

The air grew heavier. The shadows seemed to crowd closer around her, and the voice—the voice that had haunted her thoughts since she had entered this house—spoke again.

"Eliza..."

Her heart lurched in her chest, and she spun around, her grip tightening around the blade. But there was no one there. The room was still. Silent.

But the weight of the voice, the presence, was undeniable. It was real. It was here.

She stumbled backward, the knife slipping from her fingers, clattering against the floor with a sickening sound. The shadows seemed to close in, their shapes shifting, their whispers rising in volume until it was all she could hear.

"Eliza," the voice repeated, this time closer, almost in her ear. "You can never escape. It's too late."

The room seemed to tilt, the walls warping and bending around her as though the house itself was alive, swallowing her whole. Her head spun, her vision swimming with darkness, and she collapsed to her knees. The room spun around her, everything spinning into chaos as the storm outside intensified, rattling the windows like a warning.

She couldn't breathe. She couldn't think. The past had caught her, and it wasn't letting go. The truth—whatever it was—had her trapped. She was drowning in it, and there was no escape.

And in that moment, as the darkness closed in, she heard it—the final whisper, cold and unyielding.

It's time to finish what we started.

The shadows swallowed her whole.

40

The Door of the Unseen

Eliza's body trembled violently as she rose from the floor, the darkness pressing in on her from every angle. The room seemed to shrink, the walls inching closer with each breath she took. The weight of the storm outside—its howling wind, the thunder that shook the very foundations of the house—echoed in the oppressive stillness that surrounded her.

She looked down at the knife that lay at her feet. Its cold steel gleamed ominously in the dim light, and a strange, unsettling pull tugged at her as her gaze lingered on the blade. It felt familiar, as though it had always been a part of her life, a part of her family's history. And yet, it was something she had never seen, never known. The memories she had fought so hard to bury were rising once again, clawing at the edges of her mind, threatening to overwhelm her.

Her heart raced, her breath shallow as she picked up the blade. It was heavier than she expected, its presence in her hand unsettling. She could feel the weight of it deep within her chest, the very air around her thickening, as if the house itself were watching, waiting. She swallowed hard, a knot of fear and confusion tightening in her stomach.

What was happening? Her mind screamed for answers, but the words came out as nothing more than a muffled echo in the dark. The knife in her hand was a link to something—something dark, something she had been running from. She could feel it, its presence like a shadow cast across her soul.

"Eliza..." The voice again. It was deeper this time, more insistent. It came from every direction, vibrating in her chest. "You can't escape it. You can't run from your past any longer."

Her eyes darted around the room, but there was no one there. The shadows twisted, elongating, as though the darkness itself had a life of its own, wrapping itself around her. The air was suffocating now, heavy with the scent of mildew, dust, and something far worse—decay. She had to get out. She had to leave this room, this house, before it consumed her completely.

But the door was gone.

She hadn't noticed it at first, but now that she turned to look, it was simply... not there. The space where it had stood just moments ago was empty, the wall seamless, as though the door had never existed.

"Where is it?" she whispered to herself, her voice hoarse with panic.

The room seemed to warp around her, bending, twisting, as if the very fabric of reality was being torn apart. Her mind spun, and for a moment, she couldn't tell where the shadows ended and the walls began. The room was now an endless void, a vast expanse of nothingness that stretched into infinity. She could feel it—something in the air, something pulling her deeper into the house, deeper into the heart of its secrets.

"Eliza..." The voice again, closer now, so close it felt like a whisper right in her ear. "You've been hiding from it for so long. The door is always there, waiting for you. But you haven't been ready to open it."

The words hit her like a physical blow. She staggered backward, the ground beneath her feet shifting as though the very earth were unstable. She reached out for something—anything—to hold on to, but there was nothing. The walls, the floor, everything around her was in motion, as if the house itself were alive, bending to some unseen will.

"The door..." she whispered, her voice trembling. "Where is it?"

Her pulse pounded in her ears as the room seemed to shift again. The air grew colder, the shadows darker, and then, suddenly, the door appeared.

It was no longer the wooden, weathered door she had seen earlier. This door was different—newer, cleaner, its surface smooth and polished. The brass handle gleamed in the dim light, and the faintest glow of light seeped from the cracks around its edges. It beckoned her, pulling her toward it as if it were the only thing that mattered in the world.

Eliza's feet moved on their own, as though they knew where to go. She reached out for the door handle, her fingers brushing against the cold metal. The moment she touched it, a sharp jolt of energy shot through her arm, like a bolt of lightning coursing through her veins. She gasped, her body convulsing with the force of it. The door groaned, its hinges creaking as though it, too, was alive, protesting against being opened.

This is it, she thought, her breath shallow. This is the moment.

With a final, shaking breath, she turned the handle and pulled the door open.

The world beyond the door was not what she expected.

It wasn't a hallway or a room. It was an endless expanse of nothing. The air was thick with fog, and the floor beneath her feet was made of stone, cold and rough to the touch. In the distance, faint whispers echoed, distant voices that she couldn't quite make out, but their presence was undeniable.

"Eliza..."

The voice came again, but this time it was different. It was not just a voice. It was a memory, a fragment of something lost long ago. It felt like her mother's voice. But how? Her mother had been gone for so long. She had buried her memories, buried the pain, but now...

Now, it all rushed back.

She stepped forward, drawn by the voice, by the pull of the fog. She could see something ahead, something faint, just barely visible through the haze. A figure. Tall, familiar.

"Eliza…" the voice whispered again. "It's time to come home."

Her heart stopped. She knew this figure. She had known it her entire life, but she had never been able to remember it clearly, not until now. It was her father—his face so clear, so alive, yet pale and twisted in the shadows.

"You've opened the door," he said, his voice full of sorrow and something darker. "Now, you must face what's inside."

Eliza's hands clenched into fists as she stepped closer, the fog growing thicker around her. She could see the figure more clearly now, but the closer she got, the more she realized something was wrong.

Her father's eyes—once filled with love and warmth—were hollow, empty. There was nothing left of him but a shell. His presence was a void, an absence of life.

And suddenly, she understood. The door was not just a doorway to the past. It was a doorway to the truth, to the legacy that had been buried. To everything she had been running from.

Her breath caught in her throat. The truth was here.

And there was no turning back.

www.ingramcontent.com/pod-product-compliance
Lightning Source LLC
LaVergne TN
LVHW011933070526
838202LV00054B/4625